Preface

The field of Accountancy and Financial Management is pivotal in shaping the financial backbone of any organization, whether it be a small business or a multinational corporation. Mastery of these disciplines not only requires theoretical knowledge but also a keen ability to apply this knowledge to real-world scenarios. This book IGNOU Accountancy and Financial Management Previous Years Unsolved Papers, comprising previous years' unsolved papers, is a vital resource for students, educators, and professionals seeking to deepen their understanding and enhance their problem-solving skills in accountancy and financial management.

The primary aim of this compilation is to provide a comprehensive tool for self-assessment and practice. By working through these past examination questions, readers can gauge their preparedness, identify areas for improvement, and gain insight into the types of questions that frequently appear in examinations. This book encourages critical thinking and the practical application of theoretical concepts, This book is organized by year and examination session, allowing for a systematic approach to study. It is recommended that students first attempt to solve each question on their own before consulting their textbooks or notes. This method will help reinforce learning and improve retention. Educators can use these questions to challenge students in the classroom or for assignment purposes, while professionals might find them useful for revising key concepts. We thank the academic institutions and educators whose examination papers have contributed to this collection. Their dedication to maintaining high standards in accountancy and financial management education has made this compilation possible. This book is intended to be a reliable resource for those studying accountancy and financial management. We hope it helps you build a strong foundation in these subjects, preparing you for academic success and a successful career in finance.

We wish you the best of luck in your preparation and hope that this book serves as a valuable resource on your journey to success.

We would like to express our gratitude to the students and educators who have contributed to the development of this book. Their insights and feedback have been invaluable in ensuring that this compilation meets the highest standards of academic excellence. As you embark on your journey through the world of algorithms, we hope that this book will be a reliable companion in your studies, helping you to unlock the full potential of your capabilities in the field of computer science.

Table of Contents

MCS-225

Master In Computer Application (MCA)

Chapter 1: Term-End Examination, June, 2022

Accountancy And Financial Management

Time : **3** Hours

Maximum Marks : **100**

Note : (i) Attempt any five questions. **(ii)** All questions carry equal marks.

1. From the following Trial Balance of M/s Volcano and Earth for the year ending 31st March, 2022 prepare Trading and Profit & Loss Account for the year ended 31st March, 2022 IGNOUAssignmentGuru.com and Balance Sheet as on 31st March, 2022 :

Particulars (Dr.)	**Amount (₹)**	**Particulars (Cr.)**	**Amount (₹)**
Stock	48,000	Bank Loan	13,200
Building	72,000	Creditors	34,800
Debtors	51,000	Capital	96,000
Machinery	30,000	Sales	3,90,000
Drawings	12,000	Discount	1,200
Purchases	2,70,000	Purchases Returns	2,400
Insurance	4,500	Commission	2,250
Trade Expenses	10,800	Provision for Bad Debts	1,200
Sales Return	1,800	Bills Payable	6,000
Salaries	24,600		
Carriage Inwards	3,750		
Bad Debts	900		
Bills Receivable	13,500		
Cash	4,200		
Total (Dr.)	5,47,050	Total (Cr.)	5,47,050

Incorporate the following adjustments while preparing final accounts :

(i) Closing stock is valued at ₹36,000.
(ii) Provide interest on capital at 5%.
(iii) Outstanding salaries ₹2,400.
(iv) Prepaid insurance ₹450.
(v) Depreciation on building 2% and on machinery 10%.
(vi) Make a provision of 5% on debtors for bad debts.
(vii) Commission accrued and receivables ₹600.

2. Explain the following accounting concepts :

(i) Business Entity Concept
(ii) Cost Concept
(iii) Going Concern Concept
(iv) Materiality Concept

3. What are the different types of financial ratios ? Define and evaluate various solvency ratios.

4. What do you understand by cost of capital ? Explain the various constituents of 'capital' and discuss how cost of 'equity capital' is determined.

5. What do you understand by Working Capital? Discuss in detail the various sources from where working capital needs can be financed.

6. What do you understand by Receivables Management? Briefly discuss credit policy variables and explain the quantitative impact of relaxing credit standards and credit period on profits.

7. Explain the cash management cycle and discuss the motives for holding cash. Explain the Baumol's model for determining optimum cash balance.

8. Explain the nature of accounting function and discuss how accounting process acts as an 'Information System'.

MCS-225

Master In Computer Application (MCA)

Chapter 2: Term-End Examination, December, 2022

Accountancy And Financial Management

Time : **3** Hours

Maximum Marks : **100**

Note : Attempt any five questions. All questions carry equal marks.

1. From the following Trial Balance of M/s. Ocean and Island, prepare Trading and Profit & Loss A/c for the year ended 31st March, 2022 and Balance Sheet as at 31st March, 2022 :

Particulars	Dr. Amount (₹)	Cr. Amount (₹)
Plant and Machinery	3,30,000	
Fixtures and Fittings	10,320	
Fuel and Power for Factory	3,252	
Office Salaries	22,470	
Electric Expense of Factory	2,352	
Travelling Expenses	5,550	
Carriage on Sales	5,760	
Cash at Bank	13,470	
Cash in Hand	408	
Debtors	2,86,800	
Purchases	4,99,740	
Factory Wages	59,490	
Rent and Rates	10,590	
Office Expenses	16,668	
Carriage on Purchase	5,382	
Discount	2,532	
Drawings	40,920	
Stock as on 1/04/2021	1,30,350	
Manufacturing Expenses	16,080	
Sales Return	44,532	
Capital		5,59,380
Sales		7,57,062
Total	15,64,094	13,16,442

Adjustments :

i. Stock as on 31st March, 2022 is ₹99,480.

ii. Depreciate plant and machinery by 5% and fixtures and fittings by 10%.

iii. Make a provision on debtors for doubtful debts @ 21 2 %.

iv. Outstanding rent and rates ₹4.50.

v. Prepaid insurance ₹420.

vi. Outstanding wages ₹2,100 and Outstanding salaries ₹4,800.

2. Explain the following accounting concepts :

i. Dual Aspect (Duality) concept
ii. Matching concept
iii. Concept of Conservatism
iv. Consistency concept

3. What is a Cash Flow Statement? Discuss the major classification of cash flows as per AS-3 (Revised).

4. Explain the 'Operating Cycle' used for computing the working capital required. Discuss the factors influencing working capital requirements.

5. What do you understand by Capital Investment? Explain the steps involved in capital budgeting decision. Discuss the importance of capital investment decisions.

6. Briefly explain the various terms of payments adapted for business transactions. Explain credit policy variables and discuss the quantitative impact of relaxing collection efforts and increasing cash discount on profits.

7. Explain the reasons for holding inventory and discuss the objectives of inventory management. Explain the Economic Order Quantity (EOQ) approach of inventory management.

8. What is an 'Annual Report' of a company ? What kind of information is contained in this report and how is it useful to internal and external users ?

MCS-225
Master In Computer Application (MCA)
Chapter 3: Term-End Examination, June, 2023
Accountancy And Financial Management

Time : **3** Hours
Maximum Marks : **100**
Note : Attempt any five questions. All questions carry equal marks.

1. Explain the following accounting concepts : 5×4=20

(a) Business entity concept

(b) Dual aspect concept

(c) Accrual concept

(d) Matching concept

2. Discuss the various items which are shown in the Balance Sheet. Why are adjustment entries required to be made at the time of preparing Final Accounts ? Explain any such five adjustment entries. 20

3. What is a cash flow statement ? Explain the process of construction of cash flow through Direct Method. 20

4. What is an 'Annual Report' ? Explain the disclosures made in annual report and discuss the usefulness of information in annual report to internal and external users. 20

5. What are the different types of investment decisions ? Discuss the stages in capital budgeting process and explain the importance of capital investment decisions. 20

6. Explain the operating cycle concept of working capital and discuss and factors influencing working capital requirements. 20

7. What do you understand by firm's credit policy ? Discuss its important dimensions and explain the effects of liberal versus stiff credit standards. 20

8. What are the reasons for holding inventory ? Explain the traditional techniques of inventory control. 20

MCS-225

Master In Computer Application (MCA)
Chapter 4: Term-End Examination, December, 2023
Accountancy And Financial Management

Time : **3** Hours
Maximum Marks : **100**
Note : Attempt any five questions. All questions carry equal marks.

1. Explain the scope of accounting and discuss how accounting information is useful for various stakeholders of business. 20

2. Explain the following accounting concepts : 4×5=20

(a) Money Measurement Concept

(b) Cost Concept

(c) Going Concern Concept

(d) Accounting Period Concept

3. Explain the use of ratios as diagnostic tool. Discuss and evaluate various 'Solvency Ratios'. 20

4. Explain the basic four decisions which a Finance Manager has to take. Discuss the objectives of financial management and explain why wealth maximization is superior to profit maximization. 20

5. What is 'Working Capital' ? Discuss the operating cycle concept of working capital. 20

6. What do you understand by cost of capital ? Explain the various techniques used to determine the cost of equity capital. 20

7. Discuss the objectives of inventory management. Explain the Economic Order Quantity (EOQ) method of inventory management. 20

8. What are the motives for holding cash ? Explain the Baumol's model for optimum cash balance. 20

Chapter 5: Most asked Important Questions Part-A

1. What is accountancy?
Answer: Accountancy is the systematic and comprehensive process of identifying, measuring, recording, classifying, summarizing, interpreting, and communicating financial information. It helps in keeping proper track of all financial transactions of a business, ensuring transparency and accountability. Accountancy is essential for decision-making, planning, and controlling business activities. It also helps stakeholders such as investors, creditors, management, and regulatory bodies in assessing the financial health and performance of a company. The subject of accountancy includes several branches such as financial accounting, cost accounting, management accounting, and auditing. It plays a vital role in the smooth operation and growth of any organization.

2. What are the primary objectives of financial accounting?
Answer: The primary objectives of financial accounting are to systematically record financial transactions, ascertain financial results, determine the financial position, and provide financial information to various stakeholders. It ensures that all transactions are properly documented in chronological order using standardized rules and principles. Financial accounting helps in preparing financial statements such as the Profit and Loss Account and Balance Sheet. These statements provide insights into the profitability, solvency, and liquidity of the organization. The objective is also to ensure compliance with legal and regulatory requirements, provide data for planning and control, and enable external users to make informed economic decisions.

3. What are the main financial statements prepared in accounting?
Answer: The main financial statements prepared in accounting are the Balance Sheet, Profit and Loss Account (also known as the Income Statement), and the Cash Flow Statement. The Balance Sheet provides a snapshot of the company's financial position at a specific point in time, showing assets, liabilities, and shareholders' equity. The Profit and Loss Account summarizes the revenues and expenses over a period, revealing the net profit or loss. The Cash Flow Statement shows the cash inflows and outflows categorized into operating, investing, and financing activities. These statements are essential for stakeholders to assess a company's financial performance and decision-making.

4. What is the accounting equation?
Answer: The accounting equation is the foundation of the double-entry bookkeeping system. It expresses the relationship between a company's assets, liabilities, and owner's equity. The equation is: Assets = Liabilities + Capital (or Owner's Equity). This equation ensures that the balance sheet remains balanced at all times. Every financial transaction affects at least two accounts in such a way that the equation stays in balance. For example, if a business takes a loan, its assets (cash) and liabilities (loan) increase simultaneously. The accounting equation reflects the basic principle that the resources owned by a business are financed by debt or equity.

5. What do you understand by double-entry bookkeeping?
Answer: Double-entry bookkeeping is a fundamental concept in accounting where every transaction affects at least two accounts. This system ensures that the accounting equation (Assets = Liabilities + Capital) remains balanced. Each transaction involves a debit in one account and a corresponding credit in another. This dual effect provides a complete record of financial events and reduces errors. For example, when a business purchases inventory in cash, the inventory account is debited while the cash account is credited. This method provides a transparent and accurate representation of a company's financial position and helps in preparing reliable financial statements.

6. What is a ledger?
Answer: A ledger is the principal book of accounts where all transactions, after being recorded in the journal, are posted to individual accounts. It is often referred to as the "book of final entry." Each account in the ledger contains details of all transactions related to that account, which are arranged in a systematic manner. The ledger serves as the basis for preparing the trial balance and, subsequently, the financial statements. It categorizes transactions under appropriate heads such as sales, purchases, cash, bank, assets, liabilities, etc. Maintaining accurate and updated ledgers is essential for proper financial reporting and analysis.

7. What is a journal in accounting?

Answer: A journal is a book of original entry where financial transactions are first recorded in chronological order. It provides a detailed account of all transactions, including the date, accounts involved, amounts, and a brief description. Each journal entry records both the debit and credit aspects of a transaction, maintaining the double-entry system. Journals help in tracking the origin of transactions and serve as a reference for posting to the ledger. Proper journalizing ensures the accuracy and completeness of financial records. Types of journals include the general journal, sales journal, purchase journal, and cash journal, depending on the nature of transactions.

8. What is meant by debit and credit in accounting?
Answer: Debit and credit are the two fundamental aspects of every financial transaction in accounting. A debit entry is made on the left side of an account, and a credit entry is made on the right. The rules for debits and credits vary depending on the type of account. For example, in asset accounts, an increase is recorded as a debit, and a decrease is recorded as a credit. In liability and equity accounts, it's the reverse. Understanding the principles of debit and credit is crucial for recording accurate journal entries and maintaining the integrity of the accounting records.

9. What is a trial balance?
Answer: A trial balance is a statement prepared at the end of an accounting period to check the mathematical accuracy of the ledger accounts. It lists all the debit and credit balances of the ledger accounts in separate columns. The total of the debit column must equal the total of the credit column, indicating that the books are arithmetically correct. However, it does not guarantee the absence of all types of errors. A trial balance serves as the basis for preparing final accounts such as the Profit and Loss Account and Balance Sheet. It helps in identifying errors and ensuring completeness.

10. What are the types of accounts in accounting?
Answer: In accounting, accounts are broadly classified into three types: personal accounts, real accounts, and nominal accounts. Personal accounts relate to individuals, firms, and companies. Real accounts pertain to tangible and intangible assets like cash, buildings, machinery, and goodwill. Nominal accounts include all income, expenses, gains, and losses. Each account type has its own rule for debit and credit. Understanding these classifications is essential for correctly recording transactions. For instance, paying rent involves debiting a nominal account (rent expense) and crediting a real account (cash). Proper classification ensures accurate journal entries and helps maintain the integrity of financial statements.

11. What is the golden rule for real accounts?
Answer: The golden rule for real accounts in accounting is "Debit what comes in, Credit what goes out." Real accounts are those related to assets of the business—both tangible (like cash, machinery, and land) and intangible (like goodwill and patents). When a business receives an asset, the respective real account is debited because the asset is increasing. Conversely, when the business gives out or disposes of an asset, the respective account is credited. This rule helps ensure accurate entry of all asset-related transactions and plays a vital role in maintaining the financial health and transparency of the accounting records.

12. What is the golden rule for personal accounts?
Answer: The golden rule for personal accounts is "Debit the receiver, Credit the giver." Personal accounts relate to individuals, firms, and other entities with whom the business has financial dealings. If a person or organization receives value from the business, their account is debited. Conversely, if a person or organization gives value to the business, their account is credited. This rule helps ensure correct classification and recording of transactions involving third parties. For example, if goods are sold on credit to Mr. A, his personal account is debited. If payment is made to Mr. B, his account is credited accordingly.

13. What is the golden rule for nominal accounts?
Answer: The golden rule for nominal accounts is "Debit all expenses and losses, Credit all incomes and gains." Nominal accounts represent all income, expense, loss, and gain accounts that are closed at the end of the accounting period. This rule ensures that expenses and losses are recorded on the debit side, and incomes and gains are recorded on the credit side. For example, when rent is paid, the rent expense account is debited, and when interest income is earned, it is credited. These entries affect the Profit and Loss Account, which determines the net result of business operations during a period.

14. What is depreciation?

Answer: Depreciation is the systematic allocation of the cost of a tangible fixed asset over its useful life. It reflects the reduction in the value of an asset due to wear and tear, usage, obsolescence, or passage of time. Depreciation is recorded as an expense in the Profit and Loss Account and reduces the asset's value in the Balance Sheet. It helps in matching the cost of the asset with the revenue it generates, in accordance with the matching principle of accounting. Common methods of depreciation include the Straight Line Method and Written Down Value Method, based on usage and time.

15. What are the methods of calculating depreciation?
Answer: The most common methods of calculating depreciation are the Straight Line Method and the Written Down Value Method. Under the Straight Line Method, a fixed amount is charged as depreciation each year over the asset's useful life. It is simple and easy to apply. Under the Written Down Value (WDV) Method, a fixed percentage is applied on the book value of the asset each year, resulting in decreasing depreciation amounts over time. Other methods include the Units of Production Method and Sum-of-the-Years-Digits Method. The choice of method depends on the nature of the asset, its usage pattern, and applicable regulations.

16. What is a balance sheet?
Answer: A balance sheet is a financial statement that provides a snapshot of a company's financial position at a specific point in time. It lists the company's assets, liabilities, and shareholders' equity. Assets are what the business owns, liabilities are what it owes, and equity represents the owners' claim on the assets after deducting liabilities. The balance sheet follows the accounting equation: Assets = Liabilities + Equity. It is divided into two sides: one for assets and the other for liabilities and equity. The balance sheet helps stakeholders evaluate the company's financial health, liquidity, solvency, and capital structure.

17. What is a profit and loss account?
Answer: A profit and loss account, also known as an income statement, shows the revenues, expenses, and net profit or loss of a business for a specific accounting period. It begins with revenues or sales, from which all expenses (cost of goods sold, operating expenses, administrative costs, etc.) are deducted to determine the net profit or loss. The account provides insights into the operational efficiency and profitability of the business. It helps management assess the performance, control costs, and plan future activities. It is also essential for stakeholders like investors and creditors to make informed financial decisions about the business.

18. What is the difference between capital and revenue expenditure?
Answer: Capital expenditure refers to funds spent by a company to acquire, upgrade, or maintain long-term assets such as land, buildings, machinery, and equipment. These expenses are capitalized, meaning they are recorded as assets and depreciated over time. Revenue expenditure, on the other hand, includes day-to-day operational expenses such as rent, salaries, utilities, and repairs. These are recorded as expenses in the income statement and reduce the net profit of the period. The key difference lies in the duration of the benefit: capital expenditure provides long-term benefits, while revenue expenditure is consumed within the accounting period in which it is incurred.

19. What is working capital?
Answer: Working capital is the difference between a company's current assets and current liabilities. It is a measure of a company's short-term liquidity and operational efficiency. Positive working capital indicates that the company has enough assets to cover its short-term obligations, while negative working capital suggests potential liquidity problems. Current assets include cash, inventory, and accounts receivable, while current liabilities include accounts payable, short-term debt, and accrued expenses. Efficient working capital management ensures smooth business operations, timely payment to creditors, and optimal inventory levels. It also helps in maintaining financial stability and building trust with stakeholders, suppliers, and investors.

20. What are current assets?
Answer: Current assets are short-term assets that are expected to be converted into cash, sold, or consumed within one financial year or within the operating cycle of the business, whichever is longer. Common examples include cash and cash equivalents, accounts receivable, inventory, marketable securities, and prepaid expenses. These assets are essential for day-to-day operations and indicate the liquidity position of a company. Effective management of current assets ensures that the business can meet its short-term obligations and operate efficiently. Monitoring current assets helps in identifying potential cash flow problems and in taking timely corrective actions for maintaining financial stability.

21. What are current liabilities?
Answer: Current liabilities are a company's short-term financial obligations that are expected to be settled within one year or within the operating cycle, whichever is longer. These include trade payables, short-term loans, outstanding expenses, accrued liabilities, and taxes payable. Managing current liabilities effectively is critical for maintaining liquidity and operational efficiency. Companies must ensure they have adequate current assets to meet these obligations as they fall due. Failure to manage current liabilities can lead to cash flow problems, loss of creditworthiness, or even insolvency. Therefore, current liabilities are closely monitored in financial analysis and working capital management.

22. What is goodwill?
Answer: Goodwill is an intangible asset that arises when a company acquires another company for a price higher than the fair market value of its net assets. It represents non-physical assets such as brand reputation, customer loyalty, employee relations, and intellectual property. Goodwill is recorded only during a business acquisition and appears on the acquiring company's balance sheet. It is not amortized but is tested annually for impairment. If goodwill is found to be impaired, its value is reduced on the balance sheet, and a loss is recognized. Goodwill plays a crucial role in mergers and acquisitions and reflects business synergies.

23. What are contingent liabilities?
Answer: Contingent liabilities are potential obligations that may arise depending on the outcome of a future event. They are not recorded as actual liabilities in the balance sheet but are disclosed in the footnotes to the financial statements if the likelihood of occurrence is more than remote but not probable. Examples include pending lawsuits, guarantees, and warranty obligations. If the contingency becomes probable and the amount can be reasonably estimated, it should be recorded as an actual liability. Recognizing contingent liabilities is essential for presenting a true and fair view of a company's financial position and ensuring transparency for stakeholders.

24. What is accrual accounting?
Answer: Accrual accounting is a method where revenues and expenses are recognized when they are earned or incurred, regardless of when the cash is actually received or paid. This method provides a more accurate picture of a company's financial performance during a specific period, as it matches income and expenses to the same period. Accrual accounting complies with the matching principle and is preferred under Generally Accepted Accounting Principles (GAAP) and International Financial Reporting Standards (IFRS). For example, revenue is recorded when a service is rendered, not when payment is received, and expenses are recorded when incurred, not when paid.

25. What is cash basis accounting?
Answer: Cash basis accounting is a method where transactions are recorded only when cash is received or paid. Income is recognized when cash is received from customers, and expenses are recorded when cash is paid to suppliers or employees. This method is simple and often used by small businesses or sole proprietors. However, it may not provide an accurate picture of a company's financial health because it does not account for outstanding receivables or payables. It does not comply with GAAP or IFRS. Therefore, larger businesses and publicly traded companies generally use accrual accounting for more accurate financial reporting.

26. What is the difference between accrual and cash accounting?
Answer: Accrual accounting recognizes revenues and expenses when they are earned or incurred, regardless of when cash transactions occur. This method matches income with related expenses in the same accounting period, giving a more accurate view of financial performance. Cash accounting, on the other hand, records transactions only when cash is received or paid. It is simpler but may not reflect true profitability or financial position. Accrual accounting is preferred by larger organizations and is mandated under GAAP and IFRS, while small businesses often use the cash method due to its ease of implementation.

27. What is a cash flow statement?
Answer: A cash flow statement is a financial report that shows the inflows and outflows of cash in an organization over a specific period. It is divided into three sections: operating activities, investing activities, and financing activities. Operating cash flows relate to the core business operations, investing cash flows show purchases and sales of assets, and financing cash flows reflect borrowings, repayments, and equity financing. This statement helps

stakeholders understand how the company generates and uses cash, assess liquidity, and evaluate its ability to meet obligations and fund future activities. It complements the income statement and balance sheet.

28. What is the difference between gross profit and net profit?
Answer: Gross profit is the difference between a company's net sales and the cost of goods sold (COGS). It represents the profit earned directly from production or trading activities. Net profit, also known as net income, is the final profit after deducting all operating expenses, interest, taxes, and other costs from gross profit. While gross profit indicates efficiency in production and sales, net profit reflects the overall profitability of a business. Both metrics are crucial for assessing performance. Investors and managers use these figures to evaluate cost control, pricing strategies, and the company's ability to generate sustainable profits.

29. What are the components of a cash flow statement?
Answer: The cash flow statement comprises three main components: cash flow from operating activities, investing activities, and financing activities. Operating activities include cash transactions from day-to-day business operations, such as receipts from customers and payments to suppliers. Investing activities cover cash used in acquiring or disposing of long-term assets, such as equipment or securities. Financing activities reflect changes in capital structure, such as loans taken or repaid and dividends paid. These sections together provide a complete picture of how cash is generated and used, enabling stakeholders to assess the liquidity, financial flexibility, and sustainability of the company.

30. What is a bank reconciliation statement?
Answer: A bank reconciliation statement is a document that matches the cash balance on a company's books to the corresponding amount on its bank statement. The objective is to identify and explain any differences between the two records. These differences may arise due to outstanding checks, deposits in transit, bank fees, direct debits, or errors. Preparing this statement helps ensure the accuracy of cash records and detect fraud, accounting errors, or unauthorized transactions. It is typically prepared monthly and aids in maintaining reliable financial statements. Reconciliation improves transparency and internal control over financial operations.

31. What is inventory valuation?
Answer: Inventory valuation is the process of assigning monetary value to a company's inventory at the end of an accounting period. It determines the cost of goods sold and the value of inventory on the balance sheet. Common methods include First-In-First-Out (FIFO), Last-In-First-Out (LIFO), and Weighted Average Cost. Proper valuation affects gross profit and net income, as under- or overvaluing inventory can distort financial results. It is essential for tax reporting, pricing decisions, and financial analysis. GAAP and IFRS provide guidelines for selecting appropriate methods to ensure consistency, accuracy, and comparability in financial reporting.

32. What is the purpose of budgeting in financial management?
Answer: Budgeting is a financial planning process that estimates future income and expenditures over a specific period. Its purpose is to guide management in resource allocation, control spending, and ensure financial discipline. Budgets help in setting performance targets, monitoring actual performance, and taking corrective actions. They also support strategic planning by anticipating future financial needs and identifying potential risks. In organizations, budgets are used at both operational and strategic levels. Effective budgeting contributes to better decision-making, goal setting, and financial stability, making it a vital tool in financial management.

33. What is break-even analysis?
Answer: Break-even analysis determines the level of sales at which total revenues equal total costs, resulting in zero profit or loss. It helps businesses understand the minimum performance needed to avoid losses. The break-even point (BEP) is calculated by dividing fixed costs by the contribution margin per unit (selling price minus variable cost per unit). This analysis assists in pricing decisions, cost control, and evaluating the viability of a product or service. It also helps in assessing the impact of changes in costs, prices, or volume. Managers use it as a planning tool to set sales targets and manage risks.

34. What is the difference between direct and indirect expenses?
Answer: Direct expenses are costs directly associated with the production of goods or services, such as raw materials, labor, and manufacturing supplies. These expenses are easily traceable to specific cost units or departments. Indirect expenses, on the other hand, are general business costs not directly linked to production, such

as rent, utilities, salaries of administrative staff, and depreciation. While direct expenses are included in the cost of goods sold, indirect expenses are part of operating expenses. Understanding this distinction is crucial for accurate product costing, profit analysis, and effective cost control in financial planning.

35. What are financial ratios?
Answer: Financial ratios are quantitative tools used to evaluate a company's financial performance and health by analyzing relationships between financial statement items. Common categories include liquidity ratios (e.g., current ratio), profitability ratios (e.g., net profit margin), solvency ratios (e.g., debt-to-equity), and efficiency ratios (e.g., inventory turnover). These ratios help stakeholders assess a company's ability to meet obligations, generate profits, and utilize resources efficiently. They also support benchmarking, trend analysis, and investment decisions. Ratios are derived from financial statements and offer insights that raw numbers may not reveal, making them vital for internal control and external financial analysis.

36. What is the current ratio and how is it calculated?
Answer: The current ratio is a liquidity ratio that measures a company's ability to pay its short-term obligations using its current assets. It is calculated by dividing current assets by current liabilities: Current Ratio = Current Assets / Current Liabilities. A ratio above 1 indicates that the company has more current assets than liabilities, which is a sign of good liquidity. However, an excessively high ratio might suggest underutilized assets. The ideal current ratio varies by industry, but generally, a ratio between 1.5 and 2 is considered healthy. It helps creditors and investors evaluate a company's short-term financial health.

37. What is the quick ratio?
Answer: The quick ratio, also known as the acid-test ratio, is a stringent measure of a company's short-term liquidity. It evaluates the company's ability to meet its current liabilities using its most liquid assets, excluding inventory and prepaid expenses. The formula is: Quick Ratio = (Current Assets – Inventory – Prepaid Expenses) / Current Liabilities. A quick ratio of 1 or higher is typically considered satisfactory. This ratio is useful because inventory may not be easily convertible to cash in the short term. It provides stakeholders with a clearer view of a company's immediate financial position and crisis preparedness.

38. What is debt-to-equity ratio?
Answer: The debt-to-equity ratio measures the relative proportion of a company's debt and shareholders' equity used to finance its assets. It is calculated by dividing total liabilities by shareholders' equity: Debt-to-Equity Ratio = Total Liabilities / Shareholders' Equity. A high ratio indicates more reliance on debt, which could be risky, especially during downturns. A low ratio suggests conservative financing. The ideal ratio varies by industry, but generally, a ratio below 1 is considered safe. This ratio helps investors and creditors assess financial leverage, risk, and the long-term solvency of the company, making it essential for capital structure evaluation.

39. What is return on investment (ROI)?
Answer: Return on Investment (ROI) is a performance measure used to evaluate the efficiency or profitability of an investment. It is calculated by dividing the net profit from an investment by the cost of the investment: ROI = (Net Profit / Investment Cost) × 100. A higher ROI indicates a more profitable investment. ROI is widely used to compare the returns of different investments or business projects. It helps management and investors make informed decisions by identifying which initiatives yield the best returns. However, ROI should be used with other metrics for a holistic financial evaluation, as it ignores time and risk.

40. What is operating profit?
Answer: Operating profit, also known as operating income, is the profit earned from a company's core business operations, excluding non-operating income and expenses such as interest and taxes. It is calculated as: Operating Profit = Gross Profit – Operating Expenses. Operating profit reflects the efficiency of the company in managing its core activities, such as production, marketing, and administration. It is a key indicator of operational success and helps assess the company's ability to generate sustainable earnings. Investors and analysts use operating profit to evaluate management performance and compare profitability across companies within the same industry.

41. What is net worth in accounting?
Answer: Net worth in accounting refers to the total value of a company's assets minus its total liabilities. It represents the shareholders' equity or the owner's interest in the business. The formula is: Net Worth = Total Assets – Total Liabilities. Net worth reflects the financial strength and solvency of the company and is an important metric for investors, lenders, and management. A positive net worth indicates that the company's assets exceed its liabilities, while a negative net worth suggests financial distress. It is a key component of the balance sheet and helps assess long-term financial health and capital adequacy.

42. What is capital budgeting?
Answer: Capital budgeting is the process of evaluating and selecting long-term investments or projects that involve substantial financial outlay. These decisions include the acquisition of fixed assets like machinery, buildings, or launching new products. Techniques used in capital budgeting include Net Present Value (NPV), Internal Rate of Return (IRR), Payback Period, and Profitability Index. The goal is to choose investments that generate value for the organization and align with its strategic objectives. Effective capital budgeting helps businesses allocate resources efficiently, manage risks, and ensure long-term profitability and sustainability. It plays a critical role in financial planning and corporate strategy.

43. What is marginal costing?
Answer: Marginal costing is a costing technique where only variable costs are considered while calculating the cost of production. Fixed costs are treated as period costs and are not allocated to individual products. This approach helps in decision-making processes such as pricing, profitability analysis, and cost control. The contribution margin, calculated as sales minus variable costs, is used to cover fixed costs and generate profit. Marginal costing is particularly useful for short-term decision-making and evaluating the impact of changes in production volume. It is different from absorption costing, where both fixed and variable costs are included in product costs.

44. What is variance analysis?
Answer: Variance analysis is the process of analyzing the differences between planned (budgeted) and actual figures in financial performance. It helps management understand the reasons for deviations and take corrective actions. Common types of variances include material, labor, overhead, and sales variances. Variance can be favorable (actual results better than expected) or unfavorable (worse than expected). This analysis is essential for cost control, performance evaluation, and operational efficiency. It enables managers to identify inefficiencies, improve budgeting accuracy, and enhance accountability across departments. Variance analysis is a core component of standard costing and management control systems.

45. What is the time value of money?
Answer: The time value of money (TVM) is the concept that a sum of money has greater value today than the same sum in the future due to its earning potential. This principle is based on the idea that money can earn interest or generate returns over time. TVM is fundamental in financial decision-making and is used in present value and future value calculations, annuities, and investment appraisals. It emphasizes the importance of timing in financial transactions and investment choices. Understanding TVM helps businesses and individuals evaluate the worth of cash flows occurring at different times and make informed economic decisions.

46. What is a fixed asset?
Answer: A fixed asset is a long-term tangible asset used in the operations of a business to generate income. Examples include land, buildings, machinery, equipment, and vehicles. These assets are not intended for sale in the ordinary course of business and have a useful life extending beyond one accounting period. Fixed assets are recorded at cost and are subject to depreciation, except for land. They appear on the balance sheet under non-current assets. Proper management and maintenance of fixed assets are crucial for operational efficiency, long-term planning, and capital budgeting decisions. Disposal or sale of fixed assets may result in gains or losses.

47. What is amortization?
Answer: Amortization is the process of gradually writing off the cost of an intangible asset over its useful life. Intangible assets include patents, copyrights, trademarks, and goodwill. Amortization reflects the consumption of the economic benefits of the asset and is recorded as an expense in the income statement. Unlike depreciation, which applies to tangible assets, amortization is used for intangible assets. It helps in matching the asset's cost with the

revenue it generates, adhering to the matching principle in accounting. Amortization schedules can be straight-line or based on usage patterns, and it impacts financial statements and tax reporting.

48. What is an intangible asset?

Answer: An intangible asset is a non-physical asset that provides economic benefits to a business. Examples include trademarks, copyrights, patents, brand recognition, and software. These assets are valuable because they can generate revenue and enhance competitiveness, even though they lack physical substance. Intangible assets are recorded on the balance sheet when acquired externally and can be amortized over their useful life. Internally generated intangibles are often not recognized under conservative accounting practices. Valuation and impairment of intangible assets require judgment and compliance with accounting standards. They play a critical role in technology-driven and service-based businesses where intellectual property is key.

49. What is working capital management?

Answer: Working capital management refers to the administration of a company's short-term assets and liabilities to ensure efficient operations and financial stability. It involves managing cash, inventory, accounts receivable, and accounts payable to maintain adequate liquidity and avoid insolvency. The objective is to balance profitability with risk by optimizing the level of current assets and liabilities. Good working capital management ensures that the business can meet its short-term obligations and invest in day-to-day operations. Techniques include inventory control, credit policy, cash budgeting, and payment scheduling. Effective management leads to improved cash flow, operational efficiency, and financial performance.

50. What is horizontal analysis?

Answer: Horizontal analysis, also known as trend analysis, is a financial analysis technique that compares financial data over multiple periods. It involves calculating the percentage change in financial statement items such as revenues, expenses, and assets from one period to another. This analysis helps identify trends, growth patterns, and potential problem areas. For example, a consistent increase in revenue may indicate business expansion, while rising expenses may signal cost management issues. Horizontal analysis is useful for internal evaluation and external benchmarking, providing insights into performance and supporting strategic decision-making. It complements vertical analysis and ratio analysis in financial reporting.

Chapter 6: Most asked Important Questions Part-B

51. What is vertical analysis?
Answer: Vertical analysis, also known as common-size analysis, is a financial analysis method where each item in a financial statement is represented as a percentage of a base amount. In the income statement, all line items are shown as a percentage of total sales, while in the balance sheet, they are shown as a percentage of total assets. This method allows for easy comparison between companies of different sizes or between periods within the same company. Vertical analysis highlights the relative proportion of each item, facilitating trend identification, cost control, and financial performance assessment.

52. What is the purpose of financial reporting?
Answer: The purpose of financial reporting is to provide relevant, reliable, and timely financial information about an organization's financial performance, position, and cash flows to various stakeholders, including investors, creditors, regulators, and management. It helps users make informed decisions regarding investment, lending, and governance. Financial reports include the balance sheet, income statement, cash flow statement, and notes to accounts. These reports promote transparency, accountability, and comparability among companies. They are prepared in accordance with accounting standards and legal requirements, ensuring consistency and trustworthiness in financial disclosures.

53. What is bookkeeping?
Answer: Bookkeeping is the process of recording all financial transactions of a business in a systematic and chronological order. It involves maintaining accurate and complete records of receipts, payments, sales, purchases, and other financial activities. Bookkeeping serves as the foundation for accounting and financial reporting. There are two main types: single-entry and double-entry bookkeeping. Proper bookkeeping ensures that financial data is available for preparing financial statements, filing taxes, and making managerial decisions. It also helps in auditing and internal control. Bookkeepers use journals, ledgers, and accounting software to maintain records.

54. What is a contingent liability?
Answer: A contingent liability is a potential obligation that may arise depending on the outcome of a future uncertain event. It is not recorded in the accounts until the occurrence of the event becomes probable and the amount can be reasonably estimated. Examples include pending lawsuits, product warranties, or guarantees. Contingent liabilities are disclosed in the notes to the financial statements. Recognizing such liabilities helps stakeholders understand potential financial risks. They are important for risk management, financial planning, and maintaining transparency in reporting obligations that may impact the company's financial position.

55. What is GAAP?
Answer: GAAP stands for Generally Accepted Accounting Principles. It is a framework of accounting standards, principles, and procedures used in the preparation of financial statements in the United States. GAAP ensures consistency, reliability, and comparability of financial information across different organizations and industries. It encompasses principles like revenue recognition, matching, accrual, and full disclosure. Adherence to GAAP helps maintain investor confidence, ensures regulatory compliance, and improves the quality of financial reporting. In other countries, similar frameworks exist, such as IFRS (International Financial Reporting Standards). GAAP is essential for standardizing accounting practices and financial analysis.

56. What is IFRS?
Answer: IFRS, or International Financial Reporting Standards, is a set of global accounting standards developed by the International Accounting Standards Board (IASB). These standards provide a common framework for preparing financial statements across international borders, enhancing transparency, comparability, and reliability. IFRS is used by companies in over 140 countries, including those in the European Union and many parts of Asia and Africa. Key principles include fair value measurement, substance over form, and comprehensive disclosure. IFRS facilitates cross-border investments, improves financial communication, and aligns financial reporting with global best practices.

57. What is the difference between GAAP and IFRS?

Answer: GAAP and IFRS are both accounting frameworks, but they differ in several aspects. GAAP is rule-based and used primarily in the United States, while IFRS is principle-based and used internationally. GAAP emphasizes detailed guidelines and industry-specific rules, whereas IFRS allows more interpretation and professional judgment. Differences also exist in revenue recognition, inventory valuation (LIFO is allowed under GAAP but not under IFRS), and treatment of development costs. Despite their differences, both aim to provide accurate and consistent financial information. Convergence efforts have been made to bridge the gap and promote global accounting harmonization.

58. What is internal control?

Answer: Internal control refers to the policies, procedures, and practices implemented by a company to safeguard its assets, ensure accurate financial reporting, promote operational efficiency, and comply with laws and regulations. Components of internal control include control environment, risk assessment, control activities, information and communication, and monitoring. Effective internal control reduces the risk of errors, fraud, and mismanagement. It also enhances reliability in financial reporting and supports sound decision-making. Internal control systems are reviewed during audits and are essential for maintaining integrity and accountability in business operations.

59. What is an audit?

Answer: An audit is an independent examination of financial statements and records to determine their accuracy and compliance with accounting standards and regulations. It provides assurance to stakeholders that the financial information presented is true and fair. There are various types of audits, including statutory audits, internal audits, tax audits, and forensic audits. Audits help detect errors, fraud, and weaknesses in internal control. They also promote transparency, enhance credibility, and support regulatory compliance. External auditors conduct audits as per legal requirements, while internal auditors assess internal processes and controls for management use.

60. What is the purpose of cost accounting?

Answer: The purpose of cost accounting is to determine, analyze, and control the costs associated with producing goods or providing services. It helps management make informed decisions regarding pricing, budgeting, cost control, and resource allocation. Cost accounting involves techniques like standard costing, marginal costing, job costing, and process costing. By identifying cost behavior and variances, it enables businesses to improve efficiency and profitability. Unlike financial accounting, which focuses on external reporting, cost accounting is primarily used for internal decision-making. It supports performance evaluation, inventory valuation, and strategic planning within an organization.

61. What is standard costing?

Answer: Standard costing is a cost accounting technique that assigns predetermined costs to products or services, which are then compared with actual costs to determine variances. These variances help in analyzing performance and controlling costs. Standard costs are based on expected levels of efficiency and resource usage. This method allows management to identify inefficiencies and take corrective action. It also simplifies inventory valuation and budgeting. Standard costing is widely used in manufacturing industries and is essential for performance measurement, pricing decisions, and financial planning. Variance analysis under standard costing covers materials, labor, and overheads.

62. What is budgetary control?

Answer: Budgetary control is a management tool that involves comparing actual performance with budgeted figures to ensure financial discipline and control over business operations. It helps in identifying variances, analyzing their causes, and taking corrective actions. Budgetary control is a continuous process that includes setting budgets, monitoring performance, and revising budgets as needed. It supports strategic planning, resource allocation, and goal setting. Effective budgetary control enhances accountability, cost control, and overall organizational efficiency. It is used at all levels of management and is an essential part of financial management and internal control systems.

63. What is job costing?

Answer: Job costing is a cost accounting method used to determine the cost of specific jobs or projects. It is particularly useful in industries where products or services are customized, such as construction, repair services, and consulting. Each job is treated as a separate cost unit, and all related direct materials, direct labor, and overheads are recorded against it. Job costing helps in tracking profitability, controlling costs, and setting appropriate pricing for each job. It provides detailed cost information, enabling better decision-making and resource planning. Job costing also facilitates performance evaluation and cost comparison across different jobs.

64. What is process costing?
Answer: Process costing is a costing method used in industries where production is continuous and the products are indistinguishable from each other, such as chemicals, textiles, or food processing. Costs are accumulated over a period and then averaged over the units produced during that period. This method simplifies accounting by allocating costs to each process or department. Process costing helps determine the cost per unit, supports pricing decisions, and aids in inventory valuation. It also facilitates cost control and performance evaluation across different production stages. It is best suited for mass production environments with standardized processes.

65. What is overhead in cost accounting?
Answer: Overhead refers to all indirect costs incurred in the production process that cannot be directly traced to specific products or services. These include expenses like rent, utilities, administrative salaries, and depreciation. Overhead is classified into fixed, variable, and semi-variable costs. In cost accounting, overheads are allocated to cost units using appropriate bases such as labor hours or machine hours. Proper overhead allocation is essential for accurate product costing and profitability analysis. Managing overheads helps in improving efficiency, controlling costs, and optimizing resource utilization. Overhead costs are also considered in pricing, budgeting, and financial decision-making.

66. What is absorption costing?
Answer: Absorption costing is a costing method that includes all direct and indirect costs, both fixed and variable, in the cost of a product or service. It contrasts with marginal costing, which considers only variable costs. Absorption costing ensures that all manufacturing costs are absorbed by the units produced, leading to a complete view of product cost. It is required for external financial reporting under accounting standards. This method supports inventory valuation and profitability analysis. However, it may not be suitable for short-term decision-making, as it can obscure the distinction between fixed and variable costs.

67. What is break-even point (BEP)?
Answer: The break-even point (BEP) is the level of sales at which total revenue equals total costs, resulting in neither profit nor loss. It is a critical measure used in financial planning and decision-making. BEP is calculated using the formula: BEP = Fixed Costs / (Selling Price per Unit – Variable Cost per Unit). Understanding the break-even point helps businesses set sales targets, evaluate cost structures, and assess the viability of products. It is also used to analyze the impact of changes in cost or price on profitability. BEP analysis supports strategic pricing and investment decisions.

68. What is contribution margin?
Answer: Contribution margin is the difference between sales revenue and variable costs. It indicates how much revenue is available to cover fixed costs and generate profit. The formula is: Contribution Margin = Sales – Variable Costs. This margin is expressed as a total amount, per unit, or as a percentage. Contribution margin analysis is crucial for break-even analysis, cost-volume-profit (CVP) analysis, and decision-making. A higher contribution margin suggests better profitability and greater flexibility to cover fixed costs. It is used to evaluate product lines, pricing strategies, and cost control measures within the business.

69. What is working capital?
Answer: Working capital is the difference between a company's current assets and current liabilities. It represents the short-term liquidity and operational efficiency of a business. The formula is: Working Capital = Current Assets – Current Liabilities. Positive working capital indicates that a company can meet its short-term obligations, while negative working capital may signal liquidity problems. Proper working capital management ensures smooth operations, timely payments, and inventory control. It also helps in maintaining creditworthiness and financial stability. Effective management of working capital is vital for cash flow planning and business sustainability.

70. What is depreciation?
Answer: Depreciation is the systematic allocation of the cost of a tangible fixed asset over its useful life. It represents the reduction in the asset's value due to wear and tear, obsolescence, or usage. Depreciation is recorded as an expense in the income statement and reduces the asset's book value on the balance sheet. Common methods include straight-line, diminishing balance, and units of production. Depreciation affects financial reporting, tax

calculations, and investment decisions. Accurate depreciation accounting ensures true representation of asset values, supports budgeting, and aids in evaluating asset performance and replacement planning.

71. What is deferred revenue?

Answer: Deferred revenue, also known as unearned revenue, is income received by a business for goods or services not yet delivered or performed. It is recorded as a liability on the balance sheet until the revenue is earned. For example, subscription fees or advance payments fall under deferred revenue. As the company delivers the product or service, the liability is gradually converted into earned revenue. Recognizing deferred revenue accurately ensures compliance with the revenue recognition principle and provides a true view of the financial position. It helps in managing future obligations and assessing customer contracts.

72. What is prepaid expense?

Answer: A prepaid expense is a payment made in advance for goods or services that will be received in future periods. It is recorded as a current asset on the balance sheet and is gradually expensed over time as the benefit is consumed. Common examples include prepaid rent, insurance, and subscriptions. Prepaid expenses are important for matching revenues with related expenses in the correct accounting period. Proper accounting of prepaid expenses ensures accurate financial reporting, prevents overstatement of current expenses, and provides insight into upcoming financial commitments.

73. What is a trial balance?

Answer: A trial balance is a bookkeeping worksheet that lists all ledger account balances at a particular point in time. It includes debit and credit balances to ensure the accounting equation remains balanced. The purpose of a trial balance is to verify the mathematical accuracy of the books before preparing financial statements. Although a balanced trial balance indicates that total debits equal total credits, it does not guarantee the absence of errors. Errors of omission, principle, or compensating errors may still exist. A trial balance is a fundamental part of the accounting cycle and aids in error detection and correction.

74. What are accounting conventions?

Answer: Accounting conventions are generally accepted practices developed over time to ensure consistency, reliability, and comparability in financial reporting. Common conventions include consistency (using the same accounting methods), conservatism (anticipating no profit but recognizing potential losses), materiality (disclosing significant items), and full disclosure (providing all relevant financial information). These conventions complement accounting principles and guide professional judgment where formal standards may not exist. They enhance the quality of financial statements by promoting transparency and uniformity. Accounting conventions are especially important in areas where discretion is allowed or interpretations may vary.

75. What is double-entry bookkeeping?

Answer: Double-entry bookkeeping is an accounting system where every financial transaction affects at least two accounts, maintaining the balance of the accounting equation: Assets = Liabilities + Equity. Each transaction involves a debit entry in one account and a corresponding credit entry in another. This method ensures accuracy and prevents fraud by providing a complete record of each transaction. It is the foundation of modern accounting and is used universally in businesses. Double-entry bookkeeping allows for the preparation of accurate financial statements and supports internal controls and audit processes.

76. What is an accrued expense?

Answer: An accrued expense is a cost that has been incurred but not yet paid or recorded by the end of an accounting period. It is recognized as a liability and an expense in the financial statements. Examples include accrued salaries, interest, and utilities. Accruing expenses ensures compliance with the matching principle, which states that expenses should be recorded in the same period as the revenues they help generate. This practice provides a more accurate view of financial performance and supports better financial planning and budgeting.

77. What is capital reserve?

Answer: A capital reserve is a portion of a company's profits that is set aside for long-term purposes and is not available for dividend distribution. It is created from non-operating activities such as the revaluation of assets, issue of shares at a premium, or profits from the sale of fixed assets. Capital reserves are recorded in the equity section of the balance sheet and can be used for purposes like issuing bonus shares or writing off capital losses. They reflect the financial strength of a business and help in future expansion and sustainability.

78. What is revenue reserve?

Answer: A revenue reserve is a portion of a company's retained earnings set aside from operating profits for specific or general business needs. Unlike capital reserves, revenue reserves are available for distribution as dividends or reinvestment in the business. They are created to strengthen the financial position, meet contingencies, fund expansion, or repay debt. Examples include general reserve and specific reserves like dividend equalization reserve. Revenue reserves are reported under shareholders' equity and reflect prudent financial management. Maintaining revenue reserves enhances investor confidence and supports business growth.

79. What is window dressing in accounting?

Answer: Window dressing refers to the manipulation of financial statements to present a more favorable view of a company's financial position than is actually the case. It may involve timing transactions, inflating revenue, deferring expenses, or reclassifying items to improve key ratios. While not always illegal, it is considered unethical and may mislead stakeholders. Window dressing undermines the reliability of financial information and can result in regulatory penalties, reputational damage, and investor mistrust. Transparent and ethical accounting practices are essential to ensure accurate reporting and maintain stakeholder confidence.

80. What is creative accounting?

Answer: Creative accounting involves the use of accounting loopholes and discretion within legal limits to manipulate financial results. It allows companies to present financial statements in a way that meets management objectives rather than reflecting economic reality. Techniques include revenue recognition manipulation, off-balance-sheet financing, and aggressive provisioning. While it may not violate laws, creative accounting can distort true performance and mislead investors. It often precedes financial scandals and loss of credibility.

81. What is goodwill in accounting?

Answer: Goodwill in accounting refers to the intangible asset that arises when a business is purchased for more than the fair value of its net identifiable assets. It represents the value of a company's brand reputation, customer relationships, employee expertise, and other non-physical assets that contribute to future earnings. Goodwill is recorded only when it is acquired through a business combination and cannot be generated internally. It is not amortized but is tested annually for impairment. Accurate valuation and recognition of goodwill are crucial for fair financial reporting and help in assessing the long-term value of a business.

82. What is an accounting cycle?

Answer: The accounting cycle is the step-by-step process of identifying, recording, and processing a company's financial transactions to produce useful financial information. It includes steps like identifying transactions, journalizing, posting to ledgers, preparing trial balance, making adjusting entries, preparing financial statements, and closing the books. The cycle ensures systematic and accurate recording of financial data and provides a clear structure for accounting processes. Completing the accounting cycle is essential for producing reliable financial reports and ensuring compliance with accounting standards. It repeats each accounting period and forms the foundation of bookkeeping and financial reporting.

83. What is a ledger?

Answer: A ledger is a principal book in accounting that contains all the accounts of a business, where transactions recorded in the journal are posted. It is often referred to as the book of final entry. Each account in the ledger shows the beginning balance, all debits and credits during the period, and the ending balance. Ledgers are used to prepare the trial balance and financial statements. Types include general ledger, accounts receivable ledger, and accounts payable ledger. Maintaining accurate ledger accounts ensures transparency, helps track business performance, and simplifies auditing and reporting.

84. What is a journal in accounting?

Answer: A journal in accounting is the first place where financial transactions are recorded, also called the book of original entry. Each transaction is recorded chronologically with details such as date, accounts affected, amounts, and a brief description. Journals use the double-entry system, where each transaction affects two accounts with corresponding debit and credit entries. Types of journals include general journal, sales journal, purchase journal, and cash journal. Journaling ensures that no transaction is omitted and forms the basis for posting to the ledger. It is vital for maintaining accurate financial records and audit trails.

85. What is financial forecasting?
Answer: Financial forecasting is the process of estimating future financial outcomes based on historical data, current trends, and projected economic conditions. It involves predicting income, expenses, cash flow, and capital requirements. Forecasting helps in strategic planning, budgeting, and decision-making. Methods include qualitative techniques, trend analysis, regression models, and scenario analysis. Financial forecasts guide investment decisions, resource allocation, and performance evaluation. They are essential for setting realistic goals and preparing for future challenges. Accurate financial forecasting enhances business resilience, investor confidence, and long-term sustainability.

86. What is financial planning?
Answer: Financial planning is the process of determining how a business will afford to achieve its strategic objectives and manage its finances efficiently. It involves analyzing current financial status, setting financial goals, creating budgets, forecasting revenue and expenses, and outlining funding strategies. Financial planning helps in risk management, investment analysis, tax planning, and cost control. It provides a roadmap for growth, profitability, and stability. Effective financial planning aligns business operations with financial goals, enhances decision-making, and ensures optimal utilization of resources for long-term success.

87. What is fund flow statement?
Answer: A fund flow statement shows the movement of funds (working capital) between two balance sheet dates. It highlights sources and applications of funds, providing insight into financial activities that affect a company's working capital. The statement helps management understand the changes in financial position and supports long-term financial planning. Fund flow statements are useful for assessing the company's financial health, investment patterns, and funding strategies. They complement income statements and balance sheets by showing how financial resources are managed within the organization. This analysis aids in decision-making and evaluating financial efficiency.

88. What is cash flow statement?
Answer: A cash flow statement provides information about the cash inflows and outflows of a business over a specific period, classified into operating, investing, and financing activities. It helps in assessing liquidity, financial flexibility, and overall cash management. The cash flow statement is essential for understanding how a business generates and uses cash, unlike the income statement, which is based on accrual accounting. It supports internal decision-making, investor analysis, and credit evaluation. The statement also aids in forecasting future cash flows, planning capital requirements, and evaluating the company's ability to meet obligations.

89. What is a profit and loss account?
Answer: A profit and loss account, also known as an income statement, summarizes the revenues, costs, and expenses incurred during a specific period. It shows the company's operational performance and indicates whether it earned a profit or suffered a loss. Key components include revenue, cost of goods sold, gross profit, operating expenses, and net profit. The statement helps in evaluating business efficiency, profitability trends, and operational management. It is essential for stakeholders like investors, management, and lenders to make informed financial decisions and assess the viability of the business.

90. What is a balance sheet?
Answer: A balance sheet is a financial statement that provides a snapshot of a company's financial position at a specific point in time. It lists the company's assets, liabilities, and shareholders' equity, ensuring that the accounting equation (Assets = Liabilities + Equity) is balanced. Assets are resources owned, liabilities are obligations owed, and equity represents the owner's interest. The balance sheet is used to assess liquidity, solvency, and capital structure. It supports credit decisions, investment analysis, and performance evaluation. A well-prepared balance sheet enhances transparency and provides insights into a company's financial health.

91. What is accounting information system (AIS)?
Answer: An Accounting Information System (AIS) is a structure that collects, stores, processes, and reports financial and accounting data for decision-making. It integrates accounting principles with information technology

to automate and streamline financial operations. Components include people, procedures, data, software, and hardware. AIS supports transaction recording, financial reporting, budgeting, auditing, and compliance. It enhances accuracy, speed, and security in handling financial data. A well-designed AIS enables real-time financial analysis, improves internal control, and helps organizations meet regulatory and operational needs effectively.

92. What is responsibility accounting?
Answer: Responsibility accounting is a system of accounting that segregates revenue and expenses into areas of responsibility, assigning them to specific managers. It holds individual departments or units accountable for their financial performance. Responsibility centers include cost centers, revenue centers, profit centers, and investment centers. This system supports performance evaluation, budgetary control, and strategic decision-making. By promoting accountability and transparency, responsibility accounting encourages efficient resource use and motivates managers to achieve organizational goals. It is a key tool for decentralized organizations to monitor performance effectively.

93. What is zero-based budgeting (ZBB)?
Answer: Zero-based budgeting is a budgeting method where all expenses must be justified and approved for each new period, starting from a "zero base." Unlike traditional budgeting, ZBB does not assume that past budgets are a baseline. Managers must justify the necessity and benefits of every expense, regardless of previous expenditures. ZBB promotes efficient resource allocation, cost control, and strategic alignment. It encourages critical evaluation of all operations and eliminates unnecessary spending. Though resource-intensive, it enhances accountability and supports dynamic, performance-oriented financial management.

94. What is accrual accounting?
Answer: Accrual accounting is a method of recording financial transactions when they occur, rather than when cash is exchanged. Revenues are recognized when earned, and expenses are recorded when incurred, following the matching principle. This method provides a more accurate picture of a company's financial performance and position than cash accounting. Accrual accounting is required under GAAP and IFRS for most businesses. It supports financial planning, tax compliance, and performance evaluation. Accrual-based financial statements are essential for investors, regulators, and management to make informed decisions.

95. What is cash accounting?
Answer: Cash accounting records financial transactions only when cash is received or paid. It is simpler than accrual accounting and is commonly used by small businesses and individuals. Revenues and expenses are recognized based on cash flow, which can lead to timing mismatches in reporting financial performance. While easy to maintain, cash accounting may not accurately reflect the financial health of a business with significant receivables or payables. It is generally not acceptable for external financial reporting under GAAP. Cash accounting is suitable for organizations with straightforward operations and limited regulatory requirements.

96. What is a suspense account?
Answer: A suspense account is a temporary account used to record uncertain or unclassified transactions until they can be properly assigned to the correct account. It helps ensure that the books remain balanced while discrepancies or incomplete information are resolved. Suspense accounts are common during trial balance preparation or when awaiting clarifications. Once the appropriate classification is determined, entries are transferred out of the suspense account. This practice ensures transparency, supports accurate reporting, and aids in error detection and correction within the accounting cycle.

97. What is rectification of errors?
Answer: Rectification of errors involves identifying and correcting mistakes made in the accounting records. Errors may include omission, commission, principle, or compensating errors. Timely rectification ensures accuracy in financial statements and compliance with accounting principles. Errors detected before preparing the trial balance are corrected by reversing or adjusting the relevant entries. Errors found after the trial balance or financial statements require journal entries and adjustments. Accurate error rectification maintains the integrity of accounting data, supports audit readiness, and upholds stakeholder trust.

98. What is inventory valuation?

Answer: Inventory valuation is the process of assigning a monetary value to a company's inventory at the end of an accounting period. Common methods include First-In First-Out (FIFO), Last-In First-Out (LIFO), and Weighted Average Cost. The chosen method impacts cost of goods sold (COGS), gross profit, and taxable income. Accurate inventory valuation ensures proper matching of costs with revenues and fair representation of financial position. It supports decision-making, tax planning, and compliance with accounting standards. Inventory valuation plays a critical role in financial analysis and inventory management.

99. What is cost audit?
Answer: A cost audit is an independent examination of cost records and statements to verify their accuracy and ensure that cost accounting principles are correctly applied. It helps in evaluating the efficiency of cost control, production processes, and resource utilization. Cost audits are required in certain industries as mandated by law. They aid in identifying wastage, optimizing operations, and ensuring regulatory compliance. Cost audits support management in pricing decisions, budgeting, and profitability analysis. They provide transparency and accountability in cost reporting and enhance the credibility of financial information.

100. What is financial audit?
Answer: A financial audit is an independent review and examination of a company's financial statements to ensure they are accurate, complete, and in accordance with accounting standards. Auditors assess internal controls, verify transactions, and confirm that financial statements present a true and fair view of the business. Financial audits are essential for regulatory compliance, investor confidence, and lending decisions. The audit process includes planning, evidence collection, testing, and issuing an audit report. It helps detect fraud, ensure transparency, and improve governance. Audited financial statements enhance the reliability and credibility of financial reporting.

Chapter 7: Most asked Important Questions Part-C

101. What is accounting reconciliation?
Answer: Accounting reconciliation is the process of ensuring that two sets of financial records match and are accurate. This typically involves comparing internal records, such as ledger balances, with external documents like bank statements. Reconciliation helps identify discrepancies, errors, or fraudulent transactions. Regular reconciliation ensures that the financial data is reliable and up to date. It supports audit readiness, compliance with regulations, and internal control. Key types include bank reconciliation, vendor reconciliation, and intercompany reconciliation. Accurate reconciliation is essential for financial integrity and assists management in making informed business decisions.

102. What is a controlling account?
Answer: A controlling account is a summary account in the general ledger that consolidates detailed information from subsidiary ledgers. For example, the Accounts Receivable controlling account represents the total owed by all customers, while the subsidiary ledger shows individual customer balances. Controlling accounts facilitate streamlined financial reporting, reduce clutter in the general ledger, and improve internal controls. They are commonly used for receivables, payables, and inventory. Reconciling the controlling account with its subsidiary ensures data accuracy and helps detect discrepancies early, promoting transparent and effective accounting practices.

103. What is a classified balance sheet?
Answer: A classified balance sheet presents the financial position of a business by grouping assets, liabilities, and equity into meaningful categories. Assets are divided into current and non-current, liabilities into current and long-term, and equity is reported separately. This format improves clarity, aids financial analysis, and enhances comparability. It helps stakeholders assess liquidity, solvency, and overall financial health. The classified balance sheet is a preferred format under accounting standards, as it provides a structured view of resources and obligations, supporting better financial decision-making and compliance.

104. What is retained earnings?
Answer: Retained earnings are the cumulative net profits of a company that have been reinvested in the business rather than distributed as dividends. Found in the equity section of the balance sheet, retained earnings reflect the company's ability to generate profit and retain it for growth. They can be used for expansion, debt repayment, or reserves. Retained earnings provide insight into a company's profitability history and financial health. Analyzing changes in retained earnings helps assess dividend policies, reinvestment strategies, and the long-term sustainability of the business.

105. What is the matching principle?
Answer: The matching principle in accounting requires that expenses be recorded in the same accounting period as the revenues they help generate. This ensures accurate measurement of net income for a specific period. For example, if revenue is recognized from a sale in December, related costs like commissions or delivery charges should also be recorded in December. The principle enhances comparability, provides realistic financial reporting, and aligns income with associated costs. It is a fundamental aspect of accrual accounting and is crucial for reliable financial statements.

106. What is accounting conservatism?
Answer: Accounting conservatism is a principle that guides accountants to choose the solution that results in lower profits when faced with uncertainty. It emphasizes prudence and caution in financial reporting. Under this principle, potential losses are recognized immediately, while gains are only recognized when they are realized. This prevents overstating assets or income and protects stakeholders from overly optimistic projections. Conservatism improves credibility, ensures that financial statements are not misleading, and is particularly important in industries subject to market volatility or regulatory scrutiny.

107. What is managerial accounting?
Answer: Managerial accounting focuses on providing financial information to internal stakeholders, such as managers and executives, to support decision-making, planning, and control. Unlike financial accounting, which is

meant for external reporting, managerial accounting includes cost analysis, budgeting, forecasting, performance evaluation, and internal reporting. It helps managers make informed operational and strategic decisions. Tools such as variance analysis, break-even analysis, and activity-based costing are used in managerial accounting. It plays a crucial role in improving efficiency, optimizing resource use, and achieving organizational goals.

108. What is financial leverage?
Answer: Financial leverage refers to the use of borrowed funds to finance business operations or investments. It is a strategy that can increase returns on equity if the return on investment exceeds the cost of borrowing. However, high financial leverage also increases financial risk, especially if revenues decline. Financial leverage is commonly measured using ratios such as debt-to-equity and interest coverage ratio. Understanding and managing leverage is crucial for capital structure decisions, profitability analysis, and risk management. Effective use of leverage can drive growth, but must be balanced against potential insolvency.

109. What is a petty cash book?
Answer: A petty cash book is a record used to track small, routine cash expenses such as office supplies, postage, and refreshments. It is maintained under an imprest system, where a fixed amount is replenished periodically. The petty cash book includes details like date, amount, purpose, and person responsible. Proper management of petty cash helps maintain control over minor expenditures, prevents misuse, and ensures accountability. Though dealing with small amounts, the cumulative impact on expenses can be significant, making accurate recording and regular audits important.

110. What is a trial balance error?
Answer: A trial balance error occurs when the total debits do not equal total credits in a trial balance, indicating potential mistakes in the accounting process. Errors may arise from omission, incorrect ledger posting, wrong calculations, or duplication. While some errors affect the balance (e.g., transposition), others might not (e.g., wrong account used but same amount). Identifying and correcting trial balance errors is crucial for accurate financial reporting. Regular review, reconciliations, and the use of accounting software help minimize such errors and maintain the integrity of financial statements.

111. What is working capital management?
Answer: Working capital management involves managing a company's short-term assets and liabilities to ensure it has sufficient liquidity to carry out day-to-day operations. It includes managing cash, inventory, accounts receivable, and accounts payable. The objective is to ensure efficient operations, minimize the cost of capital, and maintain financial health. Proper working capital management improves profitability, reduces financial risks, and increases operational efficiency. Techniques include cash flow forecasting, inventory optimization, and credit control policies. Effective management ensures the company can meet its obligations and invest in growth opportunities.

112. What is an audit trail?
Answer: An audit trail is a chronological record that traces the details of a financial transaction from its origin to its completion. It includes source documents, journal entries, and final ledger postings. Audit trails are essential for verifying the accuracy of financial records, supporting internal audits, and ensuring compliance with regulatory standards. A strong audit trail enhances transparency, improves accountability, and deters fraud. It also aids in resolving disputes, correcting errors, and simplifying the external audit process. Modern accounting software often provides automated audit trail features.

113. What is financial ratio analysis?
Answer: Financial ratio analysis involves evaluating a company's financial performance using key ratios derived from financial statements. Common categories include liquidity ratios, profitability ratios, solvency ratios, and efficiency ratios. Examples include current ratio, return on equity, debt-to-equity, and inventory turnover. Ratio analysis helps stakeholders assess the financial health, performance trends, and operational efficiency of a business. It supports decision-making, investment evaluation, and benchmarking against industry peers. Regular analysis helps detect financial issues early and guide strategic planning and resource allocation.

114. What is capital budgeting?
Answer: Capital budgeting is the process of evaluating and selecting long-term investment projects, such as new machinery, expansion, or product development. It involves estimating future cash flows, assessing risk, and

comparing costs and benefits. Common techniques include Net Present Value (NPV), Internal Rate of Return (IRR), Payback Period, and Profitability Index. Capital budgeting ensures that resources are allocated efficiently and that investments align with strategic objectives. It plays a vital role in financial planning and helps maximize shareholder value by selecting projects that offer the highest returns with manageable risks.

115. What is accounting standard?
Answer: An accounting standard is a set of rules and guidelines for preparing and presenting financial statements. Standards ensure consistency, transparency, and comparability across organizations and time periods. In India, accounting standards are issued by the Institute of Chartered Accountants of India (ICAI), while international standards are governed by IFRS. These standards cover various aspects such as revenue recognition, asset valuation, and lease accounting. Compliance with accounting standards enhances credibility, facilitates audits, and improves stakeholder confidence. They also provide a framework for addressing complex accounting issues.

116. What is a fixed asset register?
Answer: A fixed asset register is a detailed record of all fixed assets owned by an organization. It includes information such as asset description, purchase date, cost, location, depreciation method, accumulated depreciation, and net book value. Maintaining a fixed asset register helps in tracking asset usage, ensuring physical verification, calculating depreciation, and planning replacements. It also aids in internal control and compliance with audit and tax requirements. Accurate asset tracking improves asset management efficiency and supports decision-making related to capital budgeting and insurance coverage.

117. What is the difference between capital and revenue expenditure?
Answer: Capital expenditure refers to the funds used to acquire or upgrade long-term assets such as buildings, machinery, or vehicles. These are recorded on the balance sheet and depreciated over time. Revenue expenditure, on the other hand, relates to the daily operating costs such as rent, salaries, or utilities, which are recorded in the income statement and expensed in the period incurred. Capital expenditure provides benefits over multiple periods, while revenue expenditure supports current period operations. Understanding this distinction is crucial for accurate financial reporting and investment planning.

118. What is depreciation schedule?
Answer: A depreciation schedule outlines the depreciation expense of fixed assets over their useful lives. It includes details such as the asset's cost, useful life, salvage value, depreciation method, and annual depreciation amount. The schedule helps in calculating periodic depreciation, tracking asset values, and ensuring compliance with accounting standards. It supports financial reporting, tax planning, and budgeting. A well-maintained depreciation schedule enhances transparency, aids in asset replacement planning, and simplifies audits by providing clear documentation of asset value changes.

119. What is amortization?
Answer: Amortization refers to the process of gradually writing off the cost of an intangible asset over its useful life. Commonly amortized assets include patents, copyrights, trademarks, and software. The process is similar to depreciation but applies to intangible assets. Amortization ensures proper expense matching and reflects the consumption of economic benefits. It is recorded as an expense in the income statement and reduces the asset value on the balance sheet. Accurate amortization supports compliance, financial transparency, and investment analysis.

120. What is the cost of capital?
Answer: Cost of capital is the rate of return a company must earn on its investment projects to maintain its market value and attract funds. It represents the opportunity cost of using capital and includes the cost of debt and equity. Calculating the cost of capital helps in evaluating investment decisions, capital budgeting, and financial planning. It acts as a benchmark for assessing project feasibility. A lower cost of capital improves profitability, while a higher cost may discourage investment. Weighted Average Cost of Capital (WACC) is a common measure used in analysis.

121. What is a bank reconciliation statement?
Answer: A bank reconciliation statement compares the bank balance as per the company's books with the balance shown in the bank statement. Differences may arise due to outstanding cheques, direct deposits, bank charges, or errors. Preparing a bank reconciliation helps identify discrepancies, prevent fraud, and ensure accurate cash records.

It is an essential internal control tool for cash management. Regular reconciliation ensures financial accuracy, simplifies audits, and builds confidence among stakeholders by confirming the reliability of cash balances.

122. What is inventory turnover ratio?

Answer: Inventory turnover ratio measures how many times a company's inventory is sold and replaced during a period. It is calculated as: Inventory Turnover = Cost of Goods Sold / Average Inventory. A high turnover indicates efficient inventory management and strong sales, while a low turnover may suggest overstocking or weak demand. The ratio helps assess operational efficiency, inventory policies, and working capital requirements. It is a key performance indicator in retail, manufacturing, and distribution businesses.

123. What is internal audit?

Answer: Internal audit is an independent and objective assurance activity within an organization that evaluates risk management, control, and governance processes. Internal auditors examine financial records, operational procedures, and compliance with laws and policies. Their findings help improve efficiency, identify fraud, and support strategic decision-making. Unlike external audits, internal audits are continuous and focus on internal improvements. A robust internal audit system strengthens corporate governance, enhances accountability, and ensures sustainable growth.

124. What is external audit?

Answer: An external audit is conducted by independent auditors outside the organization to provide an unbiased opinion on the truth and fairness of financial statements. It ensures compliance with accounting standards, detects material misstatements, and builds trust with investors, regulators, and other stakeholders. The process includes planning, testing, and issuing an audit report. A clean audit report enhances credibility, while a qualified or adverse opinion may raise red flags. External audits are often legally required and are critical for financial transparency and regulatory compliance.

125. What is the accrual basis of accounting?

Answer: The accrual basis of accounting records revenues and expenses when they are earned or incurred, regardless of when cash is received or paid. This method provides a more accurate picture of financial performance and position by matching income and expenses to the correct accounting period. It is mandated under most accounting frameworks like GAAP and IFRS. Accrual accounting supports better budgeting, forecasting, and performance evaluation, making it essential for most medium and large enterprises.

126. What is an income and expenditure account?

Answer: An income and expenditure account is a summary of revenues and expenses of a non-profit organization for a specific period. It is similar to a profit and loss account in commercial businesses but does not include profits; instead, it shows the surplus or deficit. Only revenue items (not capital items) are included, and it is prepared on an accrual basis. This account helps in understanding whether the organization operated within its income, managed expenses efficiently, and used funds appropriately. It is essential for transparency and is often required by donors, government bodies, or trustees.

127. What is a receipt and payment account?

Answer: A receipt and payment account is a summarized cash book for a non-profit organization that records all cash receipts and payments during a specific period, regardless of whether they pertain to the current, previous, or future accounting period. It includes both revenue and capital items. This account provides a broad overview of cash movements and is typically prepared at the end of an accounting period before the income and expenditure account. It helps in understanding the cash position and in reconciling bank balances.

128. What is a not-for-profit organization in accounting?

Answer: A not-for-profit organization (NPO) is an entity formed for purposes other than earning profits, such as charitable, religious, educational, or social causes. In accounting, NPOs use different financial statements like income and expenditure accounts, receipt and payment accounts, and balance sheets. Their main focus is accountability and fund utilization rather than profitability. Donations, grants, and membership fees are typical sources of income. NPOs follow fund-based accounting and must ensure transparency, compliance with legal norms, and proper reporting to stakeholders and regulatory authorities.

129. What is the difference between accrual and cash basis accounting?
Answer: The accrual basis of accounting records revenues and expenses when they are earned or incurred, regardless of cash flow. This provides a realistic view of financial performance and aligns with accounting standards. In contrast, the cash basis records transactions only when cash changes hands, which may misrepresent financial status. While accrual accounting offers more accurate reporting, it is complex and resource-intensive. Cash basis is simpler but limited in scope and not suitable for large or regulated entities. Businesses often switch to accrual basis as they grow or for regulatory compliance.

130. What is the role of a budget in financial management?
Answer: A budget is a financial plan that estimates income and expenditures over a specified period. It serves as a tool for planning, controlling, and monitoring financial performance. Budgets help allocate resources, set financial targets, and evaluate performance against those targets. In financial management, budgeting supports decision-making, cost control, and risk management. Variance analysis—comparing budgeted and actual figures—helps identify areas of improvement. Well-prepared budgets contribute to financial discipline, transparency, and strategic goal achievement.

131. What is variance analysis?
Answer: Variance analysis is the process of comparing actual financial outcomes with budgeted or standard figures to identify and explain deviations. Variances may be favorable or unfavorable and can arise in costs, revenues, or profits. Common types include material cost variance, labor cost variance, and sales variance. Analyzing variances helps management take corrective actions, improve planning accuracy, and enhance control over business operations. It is an essential tool in budgeting, cost control, and performance evaluation.

132. What is the going concern concept?
Answer: The going concern concept assumes that a business will continue its operations into the foreseeable future and will not liquidate or be forced to halt operations. This principle underpins financial reporting, as it justifies the deferral of some expenses and the valuation of assets based on their ongoing use rather than liquidation value. If a business is no longer a going concern, it must disclose this and prepare financial statements on a different basis. It is a fundamental concept that impacts asset valuation, depreciation, and liabilities.

133. What is the prudence concept in accounting?
Answer: The prudence concept, also known as conservatism, advises caution when making accounting judgments under uncertainty. It requires recognizing expenses and liabilities as soon as they are foreseeable, but revenues only when they are assured. This prevents overstatement of financial performance and ensures that assets are not overvalued. Prudence enhances reliability and protects stakeholders from inflated earnings or unrealistic valuations. It is a guiding principle in preparing realistic and credible financial statements, especially in volatile or uncertain business environments.

134. What is the consistency principle in accounting?
Answer: The consistency principle requires a business to apply the same accounting methods and policies from one period to another. This ensures comparability of financial statements over time and enhances reliability. If a change in method is necessary, it must be disclosed along with the reasons and its financial impact. Consistency helps stakeholders analyze trends, make informed decisions, and understand the company's performance. It also promotes transparency and supports compliance with accounting standards.

135. What is a financial statement audit?
Answer: A financial statement audit is an independent examination of a company's financial statements by a qualified auditor. The goal is to provide assurance that the statements are free from material misstatements and are prepared in accordance with applicable accounting standards. The audit includes evaluating internal controls, testing transactions, and assessing accounting policies. A successful audit culminates in an audit opinion, which may be unqualified (clean), qualified, or adverse. Financial statement audits enhance stakeholder confidence, ensure compliance, and support financial transparency.

136. What is a contingent liability?
Answer: A contingent liability is a potential obligation that may arise depending on the outcome of a future event. It is not recorded in the financial statements unless it is probable and the amount can be reasonably estimated. Common examples include pending lawsuits, product warranties, or guarantees. If the likelihood is possible but not

probable, it is disclosed in the notes to the financial statements. Recognizing contingent liabilities ensures transparency, helps stakeholders understand potential financial risks, and complies with accounting standards such as IFRS and GAAP.

137. What is a provision in accounting?
Answer: A provision is an amount set aside from a company's profits to cover a known liability or loss whose exact amount or timing is uncertain. Examples include provisions for bad debts, warranties, or legal claims. Provisions are recorded as liabilities in the balance sheet and as expenses in the income statement. They ensure that expenses are recognized in the period in which they are incurred, adhering to the matching principle. Accurate provisioning helps reflect a true and fair view of financial position and supports prudent financial management.

138. What is the dual aspect concept in accounting?
Answer: The dual aspect concept is a fundamental accounting principle stating that every financial transaction has two equal and opposite effects. For example, purchasing inventory for cash increases inventory and decreases cash. This concept forms the basis of the double-entry accounting system, where every debit has a corresponding credit. It ensures that the accounting equation (Assets = Liabilities + Equity) always remains balanced. Understanding the dual aspect is essential for accurate recording, financial analysis, and ensuring the integrity of financial statements.

139. What is window dressing in accounting?
Answer: Window dressing refers to the manipulation of financial statements to present a more favorable picture of a company's financial position than is accurate. This may involve delaying expenses, inflating revenues, or hiding liabilities. While not always illegal, it is considered unethical and can mislead stakeholders. Auditors and analysts watch for signs of window dressing, especially near the end of a reporting period. Transparency, adherence to accounting standards, and strong internal controls are essential to prevent such practices and ensure credible financial reporting.

140. What is a suspense account?
Answer: A suspense account is a temporary holding account used when there is uncertainty about where to post a particular transaction. It helps maintain the balance of the trial balance until the error or classification issue is resolved. For example, if a payment is received but the customer is unidentified, the amount is posted to the suspense account. Once the correct account is determined, the entry is reclassified. Using suspense accounts ensures the accounting process continues smoothly while maintaining accuracy.

141. What is break-even analysis?
Answer: Break-even analysis determines the point at which total revenues equal total costs, resulting in no profit or loss. It helps businesses understand how much they need to sell to cover their costs. The break-even point is calculated as Fixed Costs ÷ (Selling Price per Unit – Variable Cost per Unit). This analysis aids in pricing decisions, cost control, and financial planning. It is widely used in budgeting, project evaluation, and startup feasibility studies. Understanding break-even helps in managing profitability and operational risk.

142. What is the accounting treatment of goodwill?
Answer: Goodwill is an intangible asset that arises when a company acquires another for more than the fair value of its net identifiable assets. It reflects brand reputation, customer loyalty, and other non-physical assets. In accounting, goodwill is recorded on the balance sheet and tested annually for impairment rather than amortized. If its value decreases, an impairment loss is recognized in the income statement. Goodwill accounting ensures that the acquiring company reflects the premium paid and complies with accounting standards such as IFRS 3 and ASC 805.

143. What is the debt-equity ratio?
Answer: The debt-equity ratio measures a company's financial leverage by comparing its total debt to shareholders' equity. It is calculated as Total Debt ÷ Shareholders' Equity. A high ratio indicates heavy reliance on debt financing, which increases financial risk, while a low ratio suggests a conservative capital structure. The ideal ratio varies by industry, but maintaining a balanced ratio is crucial for financial stability and creditworthiness. Investors and lenders use this ratio to assess risk and the company's ability to repay obligations.

144. What is a journal in accounting?

Answer: A journal, also known as the book of original entry, is where all financial transactions are initially recorded in chronological order. Each entry includes the date, accounts affected, amounts debited and credited, and a brief description. Journals form the foundation for the double-entry accounting system and ensure accurate recording of all business activities. Types of journals include sales, purchase, cash, and general journals. Journals are later posted to the ledger for classification and summarization. Proper journalizing is essential for audit trails and reliable financial reporting.

145. What is a ledger?
Answer: A ledger is the principal book of accounts where all transactions from journals are posted and categorized into specific accounts. It contains information about assets, liabilities, income, expenses, and equity. Each account in the ledger has two sides—debit and credit—and reflects the cumulative balance. Ledgers are used to prepare the trial balance and financial statements. They provide a structured view of financial activities and support decision-making, audits, and regulatory compliance. Maintaining accurate ledgers is essential for financial control and accountability.

146. What is accounting ethics?
Answer: Accounting ethics refers to the moral principles and standards that guide accountants in their professional conduct. Key principles include integrity, objectivity, confidentiality, professional competence, and due care. Ethical accounting practices build trust among stakeholders and ensure accurate, fair, and transparent financial reporting. Violations can lead to legal penalties, reputational damage, and financial loss. Professional bodies like ICAI and IFAC establish codes of ethics to uphold standards. Promoting ethical behavior is essential for the credibility of the accounting profession and the stability of financial systems.

147. What is deferred revenue?
Answer: Deferred revenue, also known as unearned revenue, refers to payments received by a business for goods or services yet to be delivered. It is recorded as a liability on the balance sheet until the service is rendered or the product is delivered. Once earned, it is recognized as revenue in the income statement. Common examples include subscription fees, advance rent, and prepayments. Accurate handling of deferred revenue ensures compliance with the revenue recognition principle and reflects the true financial position of the business.

148. What is operating cash flow?
Answer: Operating cash flow is the cash generated from a company's core business operations. It is calculated by adjusting net income for changes in working capital and non-cash items like depreciation. It indicates whether a company can generate sufficient cash to maintain or grow operations without external financing. Positive operating cash flow is a sign of financial health and sustainability. It is reported in the cash flow statement and is critical for liquidity analysis, budgeting, and investment decisions.

149. What is the difference between direct and indirect cash flow methods?
Answer: The direct method lists actual cash inflows and outflows from operating activities, such as cash received from customers and paid to suppliers. The indirect method starts with net income and adjusts for non-cash transactions and changes in working capital. While the direct method provides detailed insight, it is rarely used due to complexity. The indirect method is more common and easier to prepare. Both methods are acceptable under accounting standards, and understanding them is important for analyzing a company's liquidity and operational performance.

150. What is the difference between financial accounting and cost accounting?
Answer: Financial accounting focuses on recording, summarizing, and presenting financial information to external stakeholders, such as investors, creditors, and regulators. It follows standardized formats and is governed by accounting principles. Cost accounting, on the other hand, provides detailed cost data to internal management for decision-making, budgeting, and cost control. It involves analyzing the cost of production, operations, and projects. While financial accounting is historical and compliance-oriented, cost accounting is analytical and forward-looking. Both systems are essential for comprehensive financial management and strategic planning.

Chapter 8: Most asked Important Questions Part-D

151. What is the accounting treatment for prepaid expenses?
Answer: Prepaid expenses are payments made in advance for goods or services to be received in the future, such as insurance premiums or rent. In accounting, these are recorded as current assets on the balance sheet at the time of payment. As the benefit is consumed over time, a portion is gradually expensed in the income statement through an adjusting entry. This treatment ensures adherence to the matching principle by allocating the expense to the period in which the benefit is derived. Accurate recording of prepaid expenses prevents overstatement of expenses and supports financial transparency.

152. What is a trial balance in accounting?
Answer: A trial balance is a statement that lists all the balances of ledger accounts at a particular date to check the arithmetic accuracy of bookkeeping entries. It includes debit and credit balances, and the totals of both columns must match. A balanced trial balance indicates that the books are mathematically correct, though it does not confirm the absence of all errors. It is a preliminary step in preparing final accounts and helps identify posting errors, transposition mistakes, or omissions. Trial balances aid in internal control and the preparation of accurate financial statements.

153. What is the accounting cycle?
Answer: The accounting cycle is the step-by-step process followed to record, process, and report financial transactions of a business. It typically includes identifying transactions, recording journal entries, posting to the ledger, preparing a trial balance, making adjustments, preparing adjusted trial balance, creating financial statements, and closing the books. This cycle ensures systematic and consistent financial reporting and supports accuracy, transparency, and compliance with accounting standards. Understanding the accounting cycle is fundamental for maintaining proper records and producing reliable financial statements.

154. What is a credit note?
Answer: A credit note is a document issued by a seller to a buyer to acknowledge that a certain amount has been credited to the buyer's account, usually due to returned goods, overbilling, or allowances. It serves as evidence that the customer's account has been reduced and helps correct the original invoice. Credit notes are important for maintaining accurate accounts receivable, issuing refunds, and reconciling customer ledgers. Proper use of credit notes ensures transparent business dealings, prevents disputes, and supports accurate financial reporting.

155. What is a debit note?
Answer: A debit note is a document issued by a buyer to a seller indicating that the buyer has debited the seller's account. It is typically used when goods are returned or services are unsatisfactory. A debit note serves as a formal request for a credit note from the seller. In accounting, debit notes help in adjusting purchase returns and are recorded as a reduction in accounts payable. They support accurate inventory tracking, financial reporting, and dispute resolution between buyers and sellers.

156. What is a purchase order in accounting?
Answer: A purchase order (PO) is a commercial document issued by a buyer to a seller specifying the type, quantity, and price of goods or services required. It represents a formal offer to buy and, when accepted by the seller, becomes a binding contract. In accounting, POs help track purchases, manage budgets, and control spending. They are matched with invoices and delivery receipts during the accounts payable process. Effective use of POs enhances procurement transparency, prevents fraud, and supports audit trails.

157. What is a sales invoice?
Answer: A sales invoice is a document issued by a seller to a buyer detailing the goods or services sold, quantities, prices, and payment terms. It serves as a request for payment and is an essential source document in accounting. Sales invoices are recorded in the sales journal and posted to accounts receivable. Accurate invoicing is crucial for revenue recognition, tax compliance, and cash flow management. It also provides legal proof of the transaction and helps in tracking customer payments and sales performance.

158. What is a balance sheet?

Answer: A balance sheet is a financial statement that provides a snapshot of a company's financial position at a specific point in time. It includes assets, liabilities, and shareholders' equity. The balance sheet follows the accounting equation: Assets = Liabilities + Equity. It helps stakeholders assess the company's solvency, liquidity, and capital structure. A well-prepared balance sheet supports strategic decision-making, credit evaluation, and investment analysis. It is a key component of the financial statements required by accounting standards and regulatory authorities.

159. What is a profit and loss account?

Answer: A profit and loss account, also known as an income statement, summarizes a company's revenues, costs, and expenses over a specific period to determine net profit or loss. It shows how revenue is transformed into net income and includes components such as gross profit, operating expenses, and net earnings. This statement provides insight into operational efficiency, cost control, and profitability. It is essential for performance evaluation, budgeting, and financial planning, and is used by investors, creditors, and management for informed decision-making.

160. What is accounting software?

Answer: Accounting software is a computer application that helps businesses record and manage financial transactions. It automates bookkeeping tasks such as journal entries, invoicing, payroll, and financial reporting. Examples include Tally, QuickBooks, and Zoho Books. Accounting software improves accuracy, reduces manual errors, and enhances efficiency. It provides real-time financial insights, supports compliance, and simplifies audits. Modern software often integrates with banking systems and offers features like GST filing, inventory management, and multi-user access. Using accounting software is crucial for scalable and transparent financial operations.

161. What is fund flow analysis?

Answer: Fund flow analysis is a financial tool used to assess the movement of funds within a business between two balance sheet dates. It focuses on the sources and applications of funds and helps in understanding changes in the financial position. Unlike cash flow analysis, fund flow considers both cash and non-cash elements, including working capital adjustments. It is particularly useful for long-term financial planning and assessing how business operations, financing, and investing activities affect the company's capital structure. Fund flow statements support strategic decisions by showing whether funds are being used effectively or if financial restructuring is needed.

162. What is zero-based budgeting?

Answer: Zero-based budgeting (ZBB) is a budgeting approach where every expense must be justified for each new period, starting from a "zero base." Unlike traditional budgeting, which adjusts previous budgets, ZBB requires a fresh evaluation of all expenditures, ensuring resources are allocated based on necessity rather than historical trends. This method promotes efficient resource allocation, cost reduction, and strategic alignment of expenditures. It encourages managers to identify cost-saving opportunities and eliminate redundant activities. ZBB is particularly useful in dynamic environments where organizations seek to control costs, improve performance, and ensure accountability in budget planning.

163. What is marginal costing?

Answer: Marginal costing is a costing technique where only variable costs are considered in product costing and decision-making, while fixed costs are treated as period costs. It is used to determine the marginal cost—the cost of producing one additional unit. This approach aids in pricing decisions, cost control, and evaluating profitability. It highlights the contribution margin, which is the difference between sales and variable costs, helping in break-even analysis and profit planning. Marginal costing is valuable in short-term decisions such as make-or-buy, accepting special orders, and optimizing production when resources are limited.

164. What is activity-based costing (ABC)?

Answer: Activity-based costing (ABC) is a costing method that allocates overhead costs to products or services based on the activities that generate those costs. Unlike traditional costing, which uses broad averages, ABC identifies specific cost drivers and assigns costs more accurately. It helps businesses understand the true cost of production, improve pricing strategies, and identify inefficiencies. ABC is especially beneficial in complex environments with diverse product lines. By linking costs to activities, it enables better resource management and strategic decision-making. Organizations use ABC to enhance profitability analysis and operational transparency.

165. What is cost-volume-profit analysis?

Answer: Cost-volume-profit (CVP) analysis is a financial tool used to determine how changes in costs, sales volume, and price affect a company's profit. It helps managers understand the relationships between fixed and variable costs, sales revenue, and net income. CVP analysis includes calculating the break-even point, target profit levels, and margin of safety. It aids in pricing decisions, sales planning, and evaluating the impact of cost structures on profitability. By simplifying financial modeling, CVP provides insights into operational efficiency and helps in strategic planning, especially for short-term decision-making.

166. What is standard costing?

Answer: Standard costing involves assigning predetermined costs to products or services based on expected resource usage and prices. These standard costs serve as benchmarks against which actual costs are compared. Variances between standard and actual costs are analyzed to identify inefficiencies and areas for improvement. Standard costing supports budgeting, performance evaluation, and cost control. It simplifies accounting processes by reducing the need for detailed cost tracking. Widely used in manufacturing, this method aids in setting pricing policies, forecasting expenses, and enhancing managerial decision-making through variance analysis and continuous improvement.

167. What is a cost center?

Answer: A cost center is a department, unit, or function within an organization for which costs are tracked and controlled. It does not directly generate revenue but supports core business activities, such as administration, maintenance, or HR. Managers of cost centers are responsible for managing expenses within budgetary limits. Cost centers facilitate internal control, performance evaluation, and cost management by isolating costs. By analyzing cost center performance, organizations can identify inefficiencies and allocate resources more effectively. Cost centers are integral to managerial accounting and help ensure accountability across departments.

168. What is a profit center?

Answer: A profit center is a segment or department within an organization that is responsible for generating revenue and controlling costs, thereby contributing to overall profitability. Each profit center is evaluated based on its profit performance, enabling better accountability and financial analysis. Profit centers are common in diversified businesses, where different divisions operate semi-independently. Assigning revenue and costs to specific centers helps in strategic decision-making, budgeting, and performance measurement. Profit center accounting promotes a results-oriented culture, enhances transparency, and aligns operational goals with organizational objectives.

169. What is transfer pricing?

Answer: Transfer pricing refers to the pricing of goods, services, or intellectual property transferred between divisions or subsidiaries within the same organization, particularly in multinational companies. It affects how profits are allocated among different units and countries, impacting tax obligations and financial performance. Organizations must set transfer prices at arm's length to comply with international tax regulations. Proper transfer pricing ensures fairness, avoids tax penalties, and maintains transparency in intra-company transactions. It also plays a strategic role in performance evaluation, resource allocation, and managing internal efficiencies.

170. What is responsibility accounting?

Answer: Responsibility accounting is a management control system that assigns accountability for financial performance to specific individuals or departments within an organization. It involves setting budgets and evaluating actual results against those budgets for each responsibility center—cost, profit, or investment centers. This approach promotes decentralized decision-making and encourages managers to operate efficiently within their scope of control. Responsibility accounting improves transparency, supports performance-based evaluations, and aligns individual goals with organizational objectives. It fosters accountability, motivation, and a culture of ownership, essential for effective financial and operational management.

171. What is investment appraisal?

Answer: Investment appraisal is the process of evaluating the viability and potential returns of an investment project before committing funds. It involves assessing expected cash flows, the time value of money, and associated risks. Common methods include Net Present Value (NPV), Internal Rate of Return (IRR), Payback Period, and Profitability Index. This process helps decision-makers determine whether a project aligns with financial goals and offers adequate returns compared to the cost of capital. Investment appraisal ensures rational capital allocation, minimizes risks, and supports strategic planning. It is crucial for long-term financial health and resource optimization in business.

172. What is inventory valuation?

Answer: Inventory valuation is the method used to assign a monetary value to unsold stock at the end of an accounting period. It directly impacts cost of goods sold (COGS), gross profit, and taxable income. Common methods include First-In-First-Out (FIFO), Last-In-First-Out (LIFO), and Weighted Average Cost. Accurate inventory valuation ensures correct profit measurement and compliance with accounting standards. It affects decisions related to pricing, budgeting, and stock management. Improper valuation can distort financial statements and mislead stakeholders. Therefore, businesses must consistently apply a suitable method and disclose their inventory valuation policy clearly in financial reports.

173. What is financial forecasting?

Answer: Financial forecasting involves estimating future financial outcomes based on historical data, market trends, and strategic plans. It includes projecting revenues, expenses, cash flows, and capital needs. Forecasting supports budgeting, resource planning, and risk management by anticipating financial performance under various scenarios. Tools like regression analysis, trend analysis, and financial modeling are commonly used. Accurate forecasting helps management prepare for uncertainties, make informed investment decisions, and align operational goals with financial capabilities. It is an essential component of financial planning and strategic management in both short-term and long-term contexts.

174. What is the accounting treatment for bad debts?

Answer: Bad debts refer to receivables that are unlikely to be collected from customers due to default or insolvency. In accounting, bad debts are recognized as an expense in the income statement and a reduction in accounts receivable. There are two methods to account for bad debts: the direct write-off method and the allowance method. The allowance method is preferred under accrual accounting as it estimates potential losses in advance and aligns with the matching principle. Accurate bad debt accounting ensures realistic asset valuation, enhances financial reporting credibility, and helps businesses monitor credit risk effectively.

175. What is double-entry bookkeeping?

Answer: Double-entry bookkeeping is an accounting system where every financial transaction affects at least two accounts, maintaining the balance of the accounting equation: Assets = Liabilities + Equity. Each transaction involves a debit in one account and an equal credit in another. This system enhances accuracy, transparency, and the ability to trace errors. It forms the foundation of modern accounting and supports the preparation of reliable financial statements. Double-entry bookkeeping helps businesses maintain a clear audit trail and ensures that the financial records are comprehensive and balanced at all times.

176. What is the accounting treatment of accrued income?

Answer: Accrued income is income that has been earned but not yet received or recorded by the end of the accounting period. In accounting, it is recognized as an asset on the balance sheet and recorded as revenue in the income statement. This treatment adheres to the accrual concept, ensuring income is matched with the period it is earned. Examples include interest income or rent receivable. Accrued income entries are adjusted at period-end and reversed in the next period upon receipt. Accurate treatment ensures proper revenue recognition and prevents understating assets and income.

177. What is the accounting treatment for outstanding expenses?

Answer: Outstanding expenses are those that have been incurred but remain unpaid at the end of the accounting period. They are recorded as liabilities in the balance sheet and as expenses in the income statement for the current period. This treatment follows the accrual principle, ensuring expenses are matched to the correct accounting period. Common examples include unpaid salaries, rent, or utility bills. Recording outstanding expenses accurately ensures realistic reporting of profit and liabilities, and provides a true picture of financial obligations. It also aids in planning cash outflows and financial audits.

178. What is the role of internal control in accounting?

Answer: Internal control refers to policies and procedures implemented by an organization to ensure accuracy in financial reporting, safeguard assets, prevent fraud, and ensure compliance with laws. Internal controls include segregation of duties, authorization protocols, audit trails, and regular reconciliations. They reduce the risk of errors and fraudulent activities, and enhance operational efficiency. Strong internal control systems support reliable financial statements and improve stakeholder confidence. They are also essential during audits and for regulatory compliance. A well-structured internal control framework forms the backbone of corporate governance and risk management.

179. What is accounting for lease transactions?
Answer: Accounting for leases involves recognizing the financial impact of leasing arrangements on both lessors and lessees. Under the latest accounting standards (e.g., IFRS 16), lessees must recognize most leases on the balance sheet by recording a right-of-use asset and a lease liability. Lease payments are split between interest expense and principal repayment. Lessors classify leases as operating or finance leases and account accordingly. Accurate lease accounting ensures transparency in obligations, prevents off-balance-sheet financing, and aligns with the matching principle. It enhances comparability and informs financial decision-making related to leasing vs. buying.

180. What is accounting for provisions and contingencies?
Answer: Provisions are liabilities of uncertain timing or amount, while contingencies are potential liabilities dependent on future events. In accounting, provisions are recognized in the financial statements when a present obligation exists, it is probable that outflow will occur, and the amount can be estimated reliably. Contingent liabilities, if not probable, are disclosed in the notes. Examples include warranty provisions or pending litigation. Accurate accounting for provisions ensures adherence to the prudence and matching principles. It improves transparency and risk assessment, helping stakeholders understand potential obligations and financial exposures of a business.

181. What is the difference between gross and net profit?
Answer:
Gross profit is the amount a company earns from its core operations, calculated as sales revenue minus the cost of goods sold (COGS). It indicates the efficiency of production or procurement processes. Net profit, on the other hand, is the final profit after deducting all operating expenses, interest, taxes, and other non-operational costs from gross profit. While gross profit focuses on core business activities, net profit reflects overall financial performance. Both are key indicators—gross profit aids operational analysis, whereas net profit helps assess overall profitability and is used in determining retained earnings and dividend policies.

182. What is the accounting treatment of dividends?
Answer: Dividends are distributions of profits to shareholders. When declared, dividends are recorded as a liability (dividends payable) and a reduction in retained earnings. Once paid, the cash balance is reduced and the liability is cleared. Interim dividends are recorded when declared by the board, while final dividends are recorded after shareholder approval. Dividends are not considered expenses and thus do not appear in the income statement. Their treatment affects the equity section of the balance sheet. Proper recording ensures transparency, investor confidence, and compliance with corporate laws and accounting standards.

183. What is fund flow analysis?
Answer: Fund flow analysis evaluates changes in a company's financial position between two balance sheet dates, focusing on sources and uses of funds. It highlights long-term financial movements rather than daily cash transactions. The analysis helps understand how a firm generates and uses funds for operations, investments, and financing. Unlike cash flow statements, it covers non-cash transactions such as working capital changes. Fund flow statements assist management in strategic planning, evaluating financial health, and determining long-term solvency. It is particularly useful in analyzing business expansion, debt repayment, and capital formation strategies.

184. What is the difference between accounts receivable and accounts payable?
Answer: Accounts receivable represents the amount customers owe to a business for goods or services provided on credit. It is recorded as a current asset. Accounts payable, conversely, is the amount a business owes to its suppliers or creditors for purchases made on credit, shown as a current liability. Efficient management of both is essential for maintaining liquidity. Accounts receivable affects cash inflows, while accounts payable affects cash outflows. Monitoring these ensures balanced cash flow, supports vendor relationships, and improves working capital management, contributing to financial stability and business sustainability.

185. What is a general journal?
Answer: A general journal is the primary book of original entry where all non-regular transactions are recorded chronologically. It is used to record transactions that do not fit into specialized journals such as cash, sales, or purchase journals. Entries typically include depreciation, adjustments, correcting errors, and accruals. Each transaction in the general journal contains the date, accounts debited and credited, amounts, and a brief description. Proper maintenance of the general journal ensures accurate ledger postings, strengthens audit trails, and upholds financial integrity. It is vital for comprehensive and error-free accounting.

186. What is a specialized journal in accounting?
Answer: Specialized journals are used to record recurring and similar types of transactions efficiently. Common types include the cash receipts journal, cash payments journal, sales journal, and purchase journal. These journals help streamline data entry, improve accuracy, and reduce the volume of entries in the general journal. By grouping similar transactions, they also simplify posting to the ledger. Specialized journals enhance internal control and speed up the accounting process, especially in high-volume environments like retail or manufacturing. They support better reporting, organization, and division of accounting responsibilities within a business.

187. What is the purpose of preparing a bank book?
Answer: A bank book is a subsidiary book used to record all cash transactions made through the bank, including deposits, withdrawals, interest, bank charges, and cheque payments. It helps reconcile company records with bank statements and ensures accurate tracking of bank balances. The bank book is vital for cash flow management, detecting discrepancies or fraud, and preparing bank reconciliation statements. It contributes to maintaining liquidity, ensuring payments are properly authorized and tracked, and providing up-to-date financial data. Proper maintenance supports audits, internal control, and financial decision-making.

188. What is goodwill impairment?
Answer: Goodwill impairment occurs when the carrying value of goodwill on the balance sheet exceeds its recoverable amount. This happens if the business or unit associated with the goodwill underperforms or its future cash flows decline significantly. Impairment testing is done annually or when there is an indication of decline. If impairment exists, the excess value is written off as an expense in the income statement. It reduces net income and asset values. Recognizing impairment reflects true asset worth and ensures compliance with accounting standards like IFRS and GAAP, maintaining transparency and investor trust.

189. What is inventory obsolescence?
Answer: Inventory obsolescence refers to items in stock that are no longer sellable or usable due to changes in technology, market demand, or condition. These outdated goods may still hold book value but have little or no market value. In accounting, companies must write down or write off obsolete inventory to reflect its reduced worth. This is treated as an expense in the income statement and a reduction in inventory value on the balance sheet. Addressing obsolescence improves inventory accuracy, prevents overstated assets, and enhances decision-making regarding procurement and production planning.

190. What is meant by accounting equation?
Answer: The accounting equation is the foundation of double-entry bookkeeping and states that: Assets = Liabilities + Equity. It shows that all of a company's resources (assets) are financed either by borrowing (liabilities) or through owner investment (equity). Every transaction affects this equation, ensuring that the books always remain balanced. For instance, purchasing equipment with cash reduces one asset but increases another. The equation underpins the logic behind financial statements, supports internal consistency, and reinforces accountability in financial reporting. It helps both students and professionals grasp the core structure of accounting systems.

191. What is window dressing in financial statements?
Answer: Window dressing is the practice of manipulating financial statements to present a more favorable picture of a company's financial health than what is accurate. It may involve delaying expenses, accelerating revenues, or reclassifying items. While not always illegal, window dressing is considered unethical and can mislead investors, creditors, and stakeholders. Techniques include inflating asset values, understating liabilities, or changing depreciation methods. Auditors and analysts closely examine year-end transactions for signs of window dressing.

Transparency, integrity, and adherence to standards are vital to prevent such practices and ensure reliable financial reporting.

192. What is the historical cost principle in accounting?

Answer: The historical cost principle states that assets should be recorded at their original purchase price, not current market value. This ensures consistency, verifiability, and objectivity in financial reporting. For example, land bought for ₹10,00,000 remains recorded at that value, even if its market value rises. While this may lead to understatement of asset value over time, it avoids subjective valuations. Some exceptions exist, like fair value accounting for financial instruments. The principle is widely accepted in GAAP and helps maintain audit trails and comparability of financial statements across periods.

193. What is the accrual concept in accounting?

Answer: The accrual concept requires that revenue and expenses be recorded when they are earned or incurred, not when cash is received or paid. It ensures accurate matching of income and expenses to the correct accounting period. This method provides a realistic view of financial performance and is mandated under most accounting frameworks. For example, interest earned but not yet received should be recorded as income. The accrual concept improves transparency, facilitates better financial planning, and supports compliance. It is a cornerstone of financial accounting, especially in medium to large enterprises.

194. What is a cost center in accounting?

Answer: A cost center is a specific department, function, or location within an organization where costs are tracked and controlled. It does not directly generate revenue but supports revenue-producing activities. Examples include HR, IT, or maintenance departments. Each cost center is assigned a unique code, and expenses are allocated accordingly. Tracking costs by center helps in budgeting, identifying inefficiencies, and evaluating departmental performance. Effective cost center management aids in cost control, accountability, and strategic decision-making, ensuring resources are utilized optimally and financial discipline is maintained across the organization.

195. What is the accounting treatment of scrap and waste?

Answer: Scrap and waste are residual materials from the production process. Scrap often has minimal value and can be sold or reused, while waste may have no value and may need disposal. Accounting treatment varies—scrap sale proceeds are usually credited to production cost accounts or recorded as other income. Waste disposal costs are recorded as expenses. Proper accounting ensures accurate cost of production, supports environmental compliance, and reflects actual profitability. Monitoring scrap and waste also highlights inefficiencies, aids in inventory control, and promotes sustainable business practices.

196. What is zero-based budgeting (ZBB)?

Answer: Zero-based budgeting is a method where each budget cycle starts from a "zero base," and every expense must be justified, rather than simply adjusting previous budgets. It requires detailed analysis and prioritization of expenditures based on necessity and benefit. ZBB promotes cost control, resource optimization, and efficient allocation. Unlike traditional budgeting, it discourages incremental increases without scrutiny. Although time-consuming, ZBB is effective in eliminating wasteful spending and aligning budgets with strategic goals. It is particularly useful in dynamic environments or during financial restructuring and turnaround planning.

197. What is standard costing in cost accounting?

Answer: Standard costing involves setting predetermined costs for products or services, which are then compared with actual costs to analyze variances. It simplifies budgeting and cost control by providing benchmarks for performance evaluation. Variances can be favorable or unfavorable and help identify inefficiencies or areas requiring corrective action. Common standards include material, labor, and overhead costs. Standard costing supports management in decision-making, pricing, and cost reduction strategies. It also aids in planning and operational efficiency. Though less flexible in volatile markets, it remains a foundational tool in cost accounting.

198. What is a provision for doubtful debts?

Answer: A provision for doubtful debts is an estimated amount set aside from profits to cover potential losses from uncollectible accounts receivable. It anticipates that some customers may default and aligns with the prudence and matching principles. The provision is recorded as an expense in the income statement and reduces accounts receivable on the balance sheet. This conservative approach ensures financial statements are not overly optimistic and reflect a realistic asset valuation. Regularly reviewing and adjusting provisions based on customer credit risk enhances the reliability of financial reports.

199. What is capital work-in-progress (CWIP)?

Answer: Capital work-in-progress refers to the costs incurred on fixed assets that are under construction and not yet ready for intended use. Examples include buildings, plants, or machinery being built or installed. CWIP is shown as a separate line item under non-current assets on the balance sheet. Once completed, the costs are transferred to fixed assets and depreciated. CWIP helps track project spending and ensures accurate capital allocation. It is important for project management, financial planning, and audit purposes. Proper classification prevents premature depreciation and misstatement of asset values.

200. What is the difference between tangible and intangible assets?

Answer: Tangible assets are physical, measurable items such as buildings, equipment, and vehicles. Intangible assets lack physical substance but provide value, like patents, trademarks, goodwill, and software. Both types are recorded on the balance sheet, but their accounting treatment differs. Tangible assets are depreciated over their useful life, while intangible assets are amortized. Tangibles can often be resold, while intangibles may derive value from legal rights or branding. Proper distinction ensures accurate asset classification, valuation, and compliance with accounting standards. Both are essential for operational success and financial reporting.

Chapter 9: Most asked Important Questions Part-E

201. What is financial forecasting?

Answer: Financial forecasting is the process of estimating future financial outcomes based on historical data, current market trends, and management insights. It involves projecting income, expenses, cash flows, and financial positions over a specific period. Businesses use forecasting to set goals, prepare budgets, plan investments, and assess funding needs. There are two main types: short-term (usually monthly or quarterly) and long-term forecasts (annual or multi-year). Techniques include trend analysis, regression models, and scenario planning. Accurate forecasting helps anticipate challenges, seize opportunities, and maintain financial stability. It is a vital tool in strategic planning and risk management.

202. What is horizontal analysis in accounting?

Answer: Horizontal analysis compares financial data over multiple periods to identify trends, growth patterns, and performance changes. This type of analysis helps stakeholders evaluate how items like revenue, expenses, or net income have changed year-over-year. It is typically presented in percentage terms to show the rate of increase or decrease. For example, if sales increased from ₹10,00,000 in 2022 to ₹12,00,000 in 2023, the increase is 20%. Horizontal analysis supports strategic decision-making by highlighting areas of strength and concern. It is often used with vertical analysis and ratio analysis for comprehensive financial evaluation.

203. What is vertical analysis in financial statements?

Answer: Vertical analysis involves expressing each item in a financial statement as a percentage of a base figure. In an income statement, each item is shown as a percentage of total sales, while in a balance sheet, items are shown as a percentage of total assets. This method allows for better comparison across companies or time periods, regardless of size. Vertical analysis helps stakeholders understand cost structures, profitability, and financial efficiency. It is particularly useful in benchmarking, identifying cost-intensive areas, and ensuring alignment with industry norms. It complements horizontal analysis in assessing overall financial performance.

204. What is fund flow analysis?

Answer: Fund flow analysis examines the movement of financial resources within a company during a specific period. It tracks changes in working capital by analyzing sources (e.g., equity, loans) and uses (e.g., fixed asset purchases, repayments). The fund flow statement helps assess how a company utilizes funds and whether its operations are generating adequate resources. It differs from the cash flow statement by focusing on changes in long-term funds and working capital, not just cash. This analysis supports long-term financial planning and investment decision-making by highlighting capital structure changes and internal financial health.

205. What is zero-based budgeting (ZBB)?

Answer: Zero-based budgeting is a budgeting approach where every expense must be justified for each new period, starting from a "zero base." Unlike traditional budgeting, which adjusts previous budgets, ZBB requires fresh evaluation of all expenses. Each department must justify its needs based on objectives and efficiency, promoting cost control and optimal resource allocation. ZBB encourages strategic planning and eliminates outdated or redundant expenses. However, it is time-consuming and resource-intensive. It is best suited for organizations undergoing restructuring or seeking to improve financial discipline and accountability.

206. What is the purpose of budgeting in non-profit organizations?

Answer: In non-profit organizations, budgeting serves as a financial planning and control tool. It helps allocate limited resources to mission-driven activities, estimate funding needs, and monitor expenses. Budgets guide program planning, ensure compliance with donor restrictions, and support grant applications. Non-profits often prepare operating, program-specific, and capital budgets. The budgeting process includes stakeholder involvement and emphasizes accountability and transparency. Variance analysis helps evaluate financial performance against plans. Effective budgeting ensures sustainability, donor confidence, and efficient use of public or charitable funds, aligning financial decisions with organizational goals.

207. What is the difference between hard and soft costs?

Answer: Hard costs are tangible, direct expenses related to a project, such as materials, labor, equipment, and infrastructure. These are easily quantifiable and typically involve physical assets. Soft costs, on the other hand, are indirect or intangible expenses, including legal fees, architectural services, permits, and financing charges. Both are crucial in budgeting, especially in construction and capital projects. While hard costs form the bulk of a project's budget, soft costs can significantly affect overall profitability. Accurate estimation of both ensures comprehensive financial planning and prevents budget overruns or misallocations.

208. What is a flexible budget?

Answer: A flexible budget adjusts based on actual levels of activity or production rather than remaining fixed. It is particularly useful in industries with variable demand or costs. Flexible budgeting involves identifying fixed and variable costs and recalculating budgeted figures based on actual output. This approach enables performance evaluation under different conditions and provides a realistic basis for variance analysis. It helps management adapt to changing environments, make informed decisions, and improve financial control. Flexible budgets are especially valuable in manufacturing, hospitality, and retail sectors with fluctuating operational dynamics.

209. What is standard costing?

Answer: Standard costing involves assigning predetermined costs to products or services, which are then compared to actual costs to analyze variances. It simplifies budgeting, cost control, and performance evaluation. Standard costs are typically based on historical data, industry benchmarks, and expected efficiency levels. Variance analysis helps identify deviations and their causes, such as price changes, inefficiencies, or waste. Standard costing enhances decision-making by providing benchmarks and facilitating cost optimization. It is widely used in manufacturing and service industries for financial planning, inventory valuation, and internal control.

210. What is cash budgeting?

Answer: Cash budgeting involves estimating cash inflows and outflows over a specific period to ensure sufficient liquidity. It helps organizations plan for cash shortages or surpluses, schedule payments, and maintain working capital. A typical cash budget includes projected receipts, disbursements, and opening and closing balances. It supports short-term financial management, avoids overdrafts or penalties, and guides investment of surplus cash. Cash budgeting is essential for managing daily operations, especially in small businesses and seasonal industries. Regular review and updates improve accuracy and support dynamic financial planning.

211. What is the difference between gross profit and net profit?

Answer: Gross profit is the difference between a company's sales revenue and the cost of goods sold (COGS). It reflects how efficiently a company produces or purchases goods for resale. Net profit, on the other hand, is the final profit after deducting all operating expenses, taxes, interest, and other costs from gross profit. While gross profit indicates core production or sales efficiency, net profit shows the overall profitability of the business. Net profit is often referred to as the "bottom line" and is a key indicator for investors and stakeholders. Both figures are essential for understanding financial performance.

212. What is the importance of liquidity ratios?

Answer: Liquidity ratios measure a company's ability to meet short-term obligations using its most liquid assets. Common liquidity ratios include the current ratio and quick ratio. These ratios help stakeholders assess whether a business has sufficient resources to pay off current liabilities without raising external funds. A healthy liquidity position ensures smooth operations and enhances creditworthiness. Conversely, poor liquidity can lead to financial distress or bankruptcy. Liquidity ratios are crucial for short-term financial planning, managing working capital, and evaluating operational health, especially in industries with tight cash flows or high operational expenses.

213. What is contribution margin?

Answer: Contribution margin is the difference between sales revenue and variable costs. It represents the portion of sales that contributes to covering fixed costs and generating profit. The formula is: Contribution Margin = Sales – Variable Costs. This metric helps in break-even analysis, pricing decisions, and cost control. A high contribution margin indicates better profitability and greater flexibility in managing operations. It is commonly expressed as a percentage of sales and is vital for determining the profitability of individual products, segments, or projects. Managers use it to evaluate efficiency and make informed business decisions.

214. What are intangible assets?

Answer: Intangible assets are non-physical assets that provide long-term value to a business. Examples include patents, trademarks, copyrights, goodwill, brand recognition, and software. Although they lack physical form, intangible assets can significantly influence a company's value and competitive advantage. They are recorded on the balance sheet if acquired or developed at a measurable cost. Amortization is used to allocate their cost over useful life. Unlike tangible assets, their valuation and impairment require careful judgment. Proper accounting and disclosure of intangible assets ensure transparency and help stakeholders assess the company's innovation and market positioning.

215. What is the role of inventory management in financial accounting?
Answer: Inventory management plays a crucial role in financial accounting by impacting cost of goods sold (COGS), gross profit, and working capital. Proper inventory valuation ensures accurate financial statements and reflects a company's operational efficiency. Techniques like FIFO (First-In, First-Out), LIFO (Last-In, First-Out), and Weighted Average Cost affect inventory value and tax liabilities. Excess inventory ties up capital and increases storage costs, while stockouts can result in lost sales. Regular inventory audits, turnover analysis, and technology integration improve accuracy and control. Effective inventory management aligns accounting data with business operations and supports strategic decision-making.

216. What is absorption costing?
Answer: Absorption costing, also known as full costing, is a method where all manufacturing costs—both fixed and variable—are assigned to the cost of a product. It includes direct materials, direct labor, and both variable and fixed manufacturing overheads. This method is required by accounting standards for external reporting and inventory valuation. It ensures that the full cost of production is accounted for in pricing and profitability analysis. Absorption costing provides a comprehensive view of cost structure but can sometimes obscure the impact of fixed costs in decision-making. It contrasts with variable costing, which only includes variable production costs.

217. What is variable costing?
Answer: Variable costing includes only variable production costs—direct materials, direct labor, and variable overheads—in the cost of a product. Fixed manufacturing overheads are treated as period expenses. This method helps managers understand the direct contribution of products to profit and aids in short-term decision-making like pricing, product mix, and break-even analysis. Variable costing provides clearer insights into cost behavior and profitability. However, it is not accepted for external financial reporting under most accounting standards. Despite this, it remains a valuable internal tool for managerial accounting and cost control.

218. What is the role of ethics in financial accounting?
Answer: Ethics in financial accounting is crucial for maintaining trust, transparency, and integrity in financial reporting. Accountants must adhere to principles like honesty, objectivity, confidentiality, and professional competence. Ethical conduct ensures compliance with laws and standards, prevents fraud, and protects stakeholder interests. Unethical practices like manipulation of accounts, misrepresentation, or insider trading can lead to legal consequences and damage reputation. Regulatory bodies like ICAI, IFAC, and SEBI enforce ethical codes. Promoting ethics through training, internal controls, and corporate governance strengthens public confidence and supports the long-term success of the organization.

219. What is an accounting information system (AIS)?
Answer: An accounting information system (AIS) is a structured system that collects, stores, processes, and reports financial data used by decision-makers. It integrates accounting software, databases, hardware, and procedures to manage financial transactions and records. AIS automates tasks like ledger postings, payroll, billing, and financial statement generation. It enhances accuracy, reduces manual errors, ensures regulatory compliance, and supports audit readiness. Modern AIS systems also offer features like cloud storage, real-time analytics, and cybersecurity. A well-designed AIS improves financial control, supports managerial decisions, and adapts to the growing complexity of business operations.

220. What is the role of finance in strategic planning?
Answer: Finance plays a pivotal role in strategic planning by aligning financial resources with business goals. It involves budgeting, forecasting, capital allocation, and performance analysis to support long-term growth. Financial insights help identify investment opportunities, assess risks, and prioritize projects based on return on investment (ROI). Finance ensures that strategies are financially feasible and sustainable. It also monitors progress through key

performance indicators (KPIs) and financial statements. Sound financial planning supports mergers, expansions, product development, and market entry strategies. By integrating finance with strategy, organizations achieve profitability, competitiveness, and shareholder value.

221. What is the cash conversion cycle?

Answer: The cash conversion cycle (CCC) measures the time it takes for a company to convert its investments in inventory and other resources into cash flows from sales. It includes three main components: inventory conversion period, receivables collection period, and payables deferral period. The formula is: CCC = Days Inventory Outstanding + Days Sales Outstanding – Days Payables Outstanding. A shorter CCC indicates efficient working capital management and faster cash generation. Businesses use CCC to identify operational inefficiencies and improve liquidity. It plays a crucial role in cash flow planning and can affect a firm's borrowing needs and profitability.

222. What is an accounting policy?

Answer: An accounting policy is a specific principle, rule, or practice adopted by an organization for recording and reporting financial transactions. These policies guide how financial statements are prepared in accordance with accounting standards like IFRS or GAAP. Examples include depreciation methods, inventory valuation, revenue recognition, and treatment of intangible assets. Consistency in accounting policies ensures comparability across reporting periods. If a company changes its policy, it must disclose the nature, reason, and financial impact of the change. Well-defined accounting policies ensure transparency, reduce ambiguity, and support accurate financial reporting and regulatory compliance.

223. What is financial forecasting?

Answer: Financial forecasting involves estimating future financial outcomes based on historical data, market trends, and business plans. It helps organizations anticipate revenues, expenses, cash flows, and capital needs. Forecasting supports decision-making, budgeting, and strategic planning. Common forecasting methods include trend analysis, regression models, and scenario planning. Accurate financial forecasting enables businesses to prepare for uncertainties, allocate resources efficiently, and set realistic performance targets. It is particularly useful for evaluating new projects, planning expansions, and managing risks. Financial forecasts are also critical in investor presentations and loan applications to demonstrate financial viability.

224. What is a provision for doubtful debts?

Answer: A provision for doubtful debts is an estimate of the portion of accounts receivable that may not be collected. It reflects the risk of non-payment by customers and is recorded as an expense in the income statement. The provision reduces the accounts receivable on the balance sheet, providing a more realistic view of expected collections. It adheres to the matching principle by recognizing potential losses in the same period as related revenues. Regularly reviewing and adjusting this provision improves financial accuracy, aids credit control, and supports effective receivables management.

225. What is fund flow analysis?

Answer: Fund flow analysis examines the movement of financial resources in and out of a business between two balance sheet dates. It helps understand how funds are generated (sources) and how they are used (applications). This analysis is based on changes in working capital and non-current accounts. It is used to evaluate financial strategies, investment efficiency, and operational effectiveness. Fund flow statements highlight capital structure changes, loan repayment, asset acquisition, and dividend payments. Unlike cash flow analysis, it focuses on long-term financial health and resource management. It supports financial planning and policy formulation.

226. What is zero-based budgeting (ZBB)?

Answer: Zero-based budgeting is a budgeting approach where every expense must be justified from scratch for each new period, regardless of past spending. It requires managers to build budgets based on actual needs rather than historical figures. ZBB promotes cost efficiency, accountability, and resource optimization. It is particularly useful in controlling discretionary spending, reallocating funds, and eliminating outdated activities. However, it can be time-consuming and resource-intensive. ZBB is commonly used in government and non-profit sectors, as well as in companies aiming to improve cost control and strategic alignment of expenses with goals.

227. What is responsibility accounting?

Answer: Responsibility accounting is a system that assigns accountability for financial performance to specific managers or departments. It involves setting budgets, measuring results, and evaluating performance based on areas under the manager's control. Responsibility centers include cost centers, revenue centers, profit centers, and investment centers. This system promotes decentralization, enhances performance monitoring, and supports goal alignment. Managers are evaluated only on aspects they can influence, fostering motivation and fairness. Responsibility accounting supports internal control, performance appraisal, and decision-making in complex organizations. It also helps in identifying inefficiencies and implementing corrective actions.

228. What is a fixed cost?
Answer: A fixed cost is a business expense that does not change with the level of production or sales volume. Examples include rent, salaries, insurance, and depreciation. Fixed costs remain constant over a relevant range, providing stability and predictability in budgeting. They play a critical role in break-even analysis and cost-volume-profit analysis. High fixed costs can increase operating leverage and financial risk, especially in downturns. However, they may lead to economies of scale as production increases. Managing fixed costs is essential for maintaining profitability and cash flow resilience in varying market conditions.

229. What is variable cost?
Answer: Variable cost refers to expenses that fluctuate directly with production or sales volume. Examples include raw materials, direct labor, packaging, and commission costs. As output increases, variable costs rise proportionally, and vice versa. Understanding variable costs helps in pricing, budgeting, and profitability analysis. Variable costs are essential components of contribution margin and break-even analysis. Unlike fixed costs, variable costs offer flexibility during low demand periods. Proper management of variable costs improves operational efficiency, reduces waste, and enhances competitiveness. They are critical for cost control and short-term decision-making.

230. What is capital reserve?
Answer: A capital reserve is a reserve created out of capital profits that are not available for distribution as dividends to shareholders. It includes profits from asset revaluation, premium on issue of shares or debentures, and gains from the sale of fixed assets. Capital reserves are typically used for purposes like writing off capital losses, issuing bonus shares, or financing long-term projects. They enhance a company's financial strength and support future growth. Unlike revenue reserves, capital reserves maintain the integrity of shareholders' capital and comply with legal restrictions on dividend payouts.

231. What is the purpose of financial reporting?
Answer: Financial reporting aims to provide relevant, accurate, and timely financial information to stakeholders such as investors, creditors, regulators, and management. It includes financial statements like the income statement, balance sheet, cash flow statement, and notes to accounts. The purpose is to reflect the financial performance and position of the entity, facilitate investment decisions, ensure accountability, and support regulatory compliance. Effective financial reporting promotes transparency, trust, and comparability. It is governed by accounting standards and regulatory frameworks such as IFRS, GAAP, and the Companies Act. Good reporting strengthens corporate governance and market confidence.

232. What is net present value (NPV)?
Answer: Net Present Value (NPV) is a capital budgeting method that evaluates the profitability of an investment by calculating the difference between the present value of future cash inflows and the initial investment. A positive NPV indicates that the project is expected to generate value, while a negative NPV suggests a loss. The formula involves discounting future cash flows using a required rate of return or cost of capital. NPV accounts for the time value of money, making it a reliable decision-making tool. It is widely used for comparing multiple investment options and optimizing capital allocation.

233. What is the accounting equation?
Answer: The accounting equation is the foundation of the double-entry bookkeeping system and is expressed as:
Assets = Liabilities + Owner's Equity
This equation reflects that a company's resources (assets) are financed either by borrowing (liabilities) or by the owner's investments (equity). It ensures that every financial transaction has equal and opposite effects, maintaining the balance in accounts. The equation helps in preparing financial statements, understanding financial structure, and ensuring data integrity.

234. What is the difference between operating and non-operating income?
Answer: Operating income is the profit earned from a company's core business activities, such as sales of products or services. It reflects operational efficiency and is calculated before interest and taxes. Non-operating income includes earnings from peripheral activities like interest income, dividends, asset sales, or foreign exchange gains. While operating income indicates recurring profitability, non-operating income is often irregular and not reflective of core performance. Distinguishing between the two helps in assessing sustainable earnings and evaluating the performance of operations versus incidental gains or losses.

235. What is impairment of assets?
Answer: Impairment occurs when the carrying amount of an asset exceeds its recoverable amount, meaning the asset is no longer worth its book value. This may result from physical damage, obsolescence, market decline, or poor performance. Impairment losses are recognized in the income statement and reduce the asset's value on the balance sheet. It ensures that assets are not overstated and aligns with the principle of prudence. Regular impairment testing, especially for intangible assets like goodwill, enhances financial accuracy and transparency. Accounting standards like IAS 36 and AS 28 govern impairment recognition and disclosure.

236. What is the return on investment (ROI)?
Answer: Return on Investment (ROI) measures the profitability of an investment relative to its cost. It is calculated as: ROI = (Net Profit / Investment Cost) × 100
This ratio helps assess the efficiency of capital usage and guides investment decisions. A high ROI indicates better returns, while a low or negative ROI suggests inefficiency or loss. ROI is used in project evaluation, marketing campaigns, and capital budgeting. While easy to understand, it doesn't account for the time value of money or risk, so it's often used alongside other metrics like NPV and IRR for comprehensive analysis.

237. What is revenue recognition principle?
Answer: The revenue recognition principle dictates that revenue should be recorded when it is earned and realizable, regardless of when cash is received. Under accrual accounting, revenue is recognized when the service is performed or the goods are delivered. This principle ensures accurate matching of income with related expenses and provides a realistic picture of financial performance. It is governed by standards like IFRS 15 and AS 9. Following this principle enhances transparency, comparability, and stakeholder confidence in financial reports. It is especially critical in industries with long-term contracts or deferred income.

238. What is financial restructuring?
Answer: Financial restructuring involves reorganizing a company's capital structure to improve liquidity, solvency, or profitability. It may include altering debt-equity ratios, issuing new shares, rescheduling loans, or writing off liabilities. Restructuring is often undertaken during financial distress, mergers, or strategic shifts. The goal is to align finances with business strategy, reduce financial burden, and enhance shareholder value. It can involve cost reduction, asset sales, or renegotiation with creditors. While challenging, effective restructuring can revive struggling businesses and restore financial health. It requires detailed planning, negotiation, and compliance with legal and accounting regulations.

239. What is the difference between ledger and journal?
Answer: A journal is the book of original entry where all financial transactions are recorded chronologically with narration. It ensures that every transaction is captured systematically with equal debit and credit entries. The ledger, on the other hand, is the principal book of accounts where journal entries are classified into individual accounts. Each ledger account shows the cumulative effect of all transactions relating to that account. While the journal supports accurate entry and traceability, the ledger helps in summarizing financial data and preparing trial balances and financial statements.

240. What is cost-volume-profit (CVP) analysis?
Answer: Cost-Volume-Profit (CVP) analysis studies the relationship between costs, volume, and profit to support managerial decisions. It helps determine how changes in costs and sales volume affect profit. CVP analysis includes concepts like break-even point, contribution margin, and margin of safety. It aids in pricing, budgeting, sales planning, and cost control. CVP assumes constant selling price, fixed costs, and linear relationships.

9 789369 729036

Printed at Repro India Ltd.